101 QUESTIONS STUDENTS ASK ABOUT COOKING

JOY MAY

NOSH
BOOKS.COM

Contents

budgets and equipment   8

shopping   26

freezing and defrosting   30

food hygiene   34

healthy eating   54

vegetables   72

rice and pasta   84

eggs   88

how to cook things   98

how long to cook things   122

sauces   130

when things go wrong...   138

making life easier while cooking   144

miscellaneous questions   156

silly questions   174

index

Joy May

I studied Art and Design at Loughborough College of Art and Design. Among other things, I now use my creativity to write cookbooks. I have been married to Ron for over 30 years, and we have two sons, Ben and Tim, who have now graduated from Uni.

When my sister and I were quite young, probably five and six years old, we started to cook; mainly cakes, biscuits and simple meals. By the time I was twelve, we could cook Sunday lunch. I love this heritage and am passionate about good food. There is nothing I like better than a house full of people to feed.

Other books by Joy May

"Nosh 4 Students"

"Vegetarian Nosh 4 Students"

"Nosh for Graduates"

Introduction to 101

I am passionate about getting young people to cook. Things that stop them are a lack of confidence and too many unanswered questions in their heads, for example, "how do I cook this?", "how long can I keep this before it kills me?". I was fortunate enough to have been taught to cook while I was still a child. Confidence was not an issue and many of the questions were answered at that point. Fear not! Even if you have left home and cannot yet cook, that confidence you need can be quickly gained.

We asked hundreds of students what they wanted to know about cooking. We wanted the kind of questions that were most important to them, but which, due to embarrassment, they might not have asked. This book will, hopefully, answer some of the most frequently asked ones and take the fear away from 'having a go' at cooking for themselves.

I hope that these answers will take the mystery out of cooking and inspire more of you to venture out and cook some lovely, healthy meals. Hopefully, you will not resort to an endless stream of ready-made meals, takeaways, boring stuff on toast and jars of cook-in sauces, but rather, you will try your hand at the 'real thing'.

Question 1

"How do you cook?"

Alex Ferguson

Alex, this is a good question. When I learned to cook I was taught how to make specific dishes and would cook them over and over again. This repetition took all the fear from making that particular dish and gave me confidence to try the next one.

If you have absolutely no cooking experience at all, then I suggest you get a good, simple, recipe book. Don't try making complicated things, even though they may look good in the book. I wrote 'Nosh 4 Students' in order to get Ben, my oldest son, cooking. The recipes in the book are rated according to how easy they are to make. Begin with very simple recipes, something like Vegetable Soup (see page 108) or Spaghetti Bolognese (see "Nosh4students book). Once you are comfortable with those, begin to expand your repertoire and, over time, start to attempt more daring dishes.

Confidence is soon gained by a few successes and by realizing how easy cooking can be.

Question 2

"Why cook from raw ingredients when one can buy tasty, relatively healthy, ready meals?"

Anthony Scott

I love this question, Anthony. I am passionate about good food and cooking from fresh ingredients. So rather than just tell you my opinion, I did a little test.

I bought a ready-made Spaghetti Bolognese from a well known supermarket and paid £1.99 for a portion for one. I then made a Spaghetti Bolognese from fresh ingredients. This cost me £1.43 per person. So straight away you are saving 50p per person, which, over a whole semester, will start to add up.

The test continues though. I put the meals on two plates and invited four people to taste them and tell me what they thought, without telling them which was which. They did not know what they were testing or why. The ready-made meal looked very appetizing; its colour was much deeper and richer than the home-made version. However, this is where the ready-made meal peaked.

When the 'testers' tasted them, this is what they said. The ready-made version, they said, tasted bitter, bland, nasty, 'plasticy'. They couldn't taste the meat. It was stodgy and had an unpleasant aftertaste. They all said that it looked as though it should have tasted better, but did not.

The home-made version, they said, had a greater depth of flavour, tasted light and fresh, wholesome and more authentic.

The results of the test came in the form of one empty plate (the home-made one) and a half-eaten meal that ended up in the bin.

So, on the basis of taste and budget, I would recommend getting into the habit and enjoyment of cooking. The range of ready-made dinners is fairly limited when weighed against the myriad of options which you can cook.

I ALWAYS PREFER THE REAL STUFF

Budgets & Equipment

I have received many questions regarding the cost of things and how to budget etc. There are ways generally to minimize your costs:

Share the preparation of meals with a friend, so you cook one day and they cook the next. This saves time and money. You are not left with half-used tins of tomatoes etc. in the fridge.

Make enough on one day to give you a meal the next day.

If you budget for a whole month, this gives an opportunity to buy foods that are on special offer at the supermarket. Put them in the freezer until you need them.

Make a menu-plan for the whole week and only buy the foods you need for those recipes. This means excess food is not wasted, because it goes off before you can use it.

Get your parents to buy you good, quality pans and utensils. They should last through your student days and you won't be buying new ones over and over again. Tim's pans lasted throughout his Uni days, which meant he had good stuff wherever he lived.

All prices quoted in this section are at the time of writing and may vary.

Question 3

> "What equipment is essential when cooking?"
>
> *James Black*

> "What are the best basic utensils to buy?"
>
> *Claire Sampson*

> "What are the main tools I need to cook with?"
>
> *Charlotte Ironside*

> "Essential cooking kit, on a budget - I literally turned up to Uni with NOTHING, (I thought we were in catered accommodation - turns out not) so had to go out and find what I could..."
>
> *Dan Richter*

All you need is:

- 1 largish and 1 medium saucepan with lids
- 1 non-stick frying pan
- a wok is useful
- 1 non-stick baking tray
- 1 medium bowl to mix things in
- wooden spoons or Teflon spatulas
- chopping board
- fish slice (slotted turner)
- 1 colander
- sharp knife
- casserole with lid
- cheese grater
- 2 plates
- 1 cereal bowl
- 2 mugs
- knives, forks and spoons

Question 4

"How much would you recommend spending on pots and pans?" *Jack Josse*

You really get what you pay for. You can get what appears to be good value from some places, i.e. a big box containing lots of different types of pots and pans, some of which you may never use. If you buy cheap pans, the 'non-stick' will soon wear off. These pans are often quite thin, which will mean they won't have an 'even' heat across the bottom of the pan and you will tend to burn things as you cook in them.

"Should students buy quality cooking utensils. If so how much should you be spending?" *Reece Taylor*

It is best to buy reasonable quality utensils, but ones not too expensive. Bear in mind that you will be sharing your kitchen space and others may not be as careful as you. If you buy non-stick pans, be careful that you and your housemates do not use metal utensils with them.

Ikea is good for things like plates and bowls, mugs etc. I would recommend that you buy the saucepans, frying pan and wok from either Sainsburys or Tesco, as the quality tends to be good and their prices are still quite reasonable.

1 x 16 cm non-stick saucepan, 1 x 18 cm non-stick saucepan, both with lids. 1 Teflon frying pan, 1 non-stick baking tray, 1 chopping board, 1 wok and 1 x 5 piece utensil set. These are all of good quality, but you wouldn't be too upset if your housemates ruined one item.
Approx cost £80

A reasonable, sharp knife. A sharp knife takes all the effort out of chopping and slicing. You can get a good cook's knife from John Lewis. Remember to buy a sharpener at the same time. See page 14 for details.
Approx cost £16

A casserole dish, plates, cereal bowl and 2 mugs from Ikea or Dunhelm Mill. Both places have some fun stuff.
Approx cost £12 - £13

A set of knives and forks etc (24 pieces) from Ikea. You can go to Dunhelm Mill and buy them individually for much less.
Approx cost £20 from Ikea

> "Can you get non-stick pans that are not damaged by metal cutlery and cooking tools?"
> *John Cleland*

John, you can buy a Swiss Diamond pan, costing about £75. It claims that you can use metal implements. The cheaper solution is to get a good one in a supermarket for about £15 and use wooden spoons or silicon tongs and spoons.

Question 5

> "How do you sharpen a knife?" *Nakul Pande*
>
> "How often should you sharpen a knife?"
> *Abigail Wilson*

There are lots of ways to sharpen knives, involving various gadgets and 'gizmos'. There are two basic things you need to be able to do: sharpen and hone. Sharpening is something you don't need to do very often and only if the knife feels blunt. Your housemate might have tried opening a tin can with it, or something equally ridiculous! Honing is something you should do every session you use the knife. Honing is a very fine sharpening process that gives an already sharp knife an even sharper edge.

When you buy a particular knife, ask the shopkeeper which method is best for your knife. You can either use a steel or a sharpening wheel. A wheel is easier.

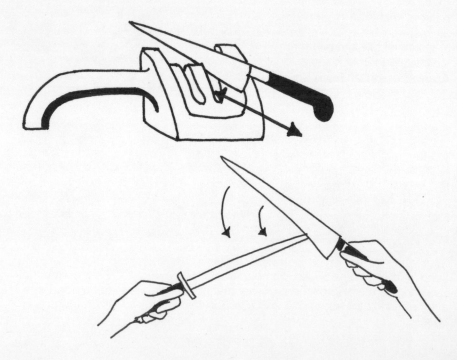

Question 6

I have sketched out a weekly menu and shopping list. (Recipes are taken from "Nosh 4 Students").

Monday	Hawaiian Risotto
Tuesday	Mince Hot Pot
Wednesday	Eat leftovers of Mince Hot Pot
Thursday	Roast Chicken
Friday	Eat leftovers of Roast Chicken with baked potato
Saturday	Spaghetti Bolognese
Sunday	Eat leftovers of Spaghetti Bolognese

This is eating really well and healthily and costs, on average, (between Tesco and Sainsburys) £29 for the week.

Jack, if you intersperse these dishes with the odd beans on toast or soup and bread, you can save a little more.

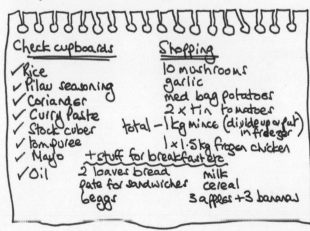

Question 7

> **"How much on average does it cost to cook a meal from scratch?"** *Emily Swallow*

Spaghetti Bolognese costs approximately £1.48 per person

Vegetable Soup costs approximately £1.20 per person

Baked Potato with Cheese costs 70p - £1 per person, depending on the cheese you use.

> **"On average, how much should you spend per meal?"** *James Taylor*

Really, it depends on how much money you have James! It is best to have a budget and stick to it. So, for instance, if you set yourself £30 per week, this needs to cover the basics of milk, cereal, tea, coffee, bread etc., as well as the main meals. You could spend £20, averaging £2.86 per day on the main meals, leaving £10 for the basics.

One way for money to go really fast is if you buy lunch out every day. A BLT sandwich, packet of crisps and a drink from Sainsbury's can on average cost £2.74 (a good average price). If you do this every day, even Monday to Friday, it will rip a £13.70 hole in your budget. If you buy sandwiches from a local store, they may cost you even more. Make your own sandwiches and buy the crisps and drinks in bulk. You will find it much cheaper.

Question 8

"What can I cook that looks impressive but doesn't cost much?" *Josh Clements*

Here is one idea, Josh. It will cost approximately **£4.18 for 2 people.**

Sweet and Sour Chicken

Serves 2

Sweet and Sour Sauce

- 2 tablespoons **tomato purée**
- 3 tablespoons **sugar**
- 2 tablespoons **white wine vinegar**
- 1 tablespoon **soy sauce**
- 2 teaspoons **cornflour**
- 1 mug **water**

- **butter** or **oil** for frying
- 1 **onion**, chopped
- 1 clove **garlic**, chopped finely
- 4 **mushrooms**, sliced
- ½ **red pepper**, sliced into long strips
- 2 **chicken breasts**, cut into pieces

1. Put the rice on to cook (see page 86).
2. To make the sauce, put all the sauce ingredients in a saucepan, apart from the cornflour. Bring to the boil, stirring well. Mix the cornflour with a little cold water and pour into the sauce, stirring as you do. The sauce should thicken. Leave the sauce off the heat until you have cooked the chicken.
3. Fry the onion, garlic, mushrooms and pepper for 1 minute. Add the chicken pieces and cook for another 3 - 4 minutes, stirring frequently.
4. Add the sweet and sour sauce to the pan. Bring to the boil, turn down the heat and simmer for 2 minutes.
5. Serve with rice.

Even the finest meal you can make will feel ordinary if it is eaten on your lap in front of the TV. Try to make an effort and sit down at a table if you have one and make it look nice with candles. The details will make all the difference!

Question 9

> ## "What are the cheapest cuts of meat to buy?"
> *A Merrick*

The cheapest cuts of meat to buy are **pork shoulder** at £2.79 per Kg, **lamb shoulder** at £4.98 per Kg and **beef brisket** at £5.48 per Kg.

All these need to be slow-cooked. The recipe on page 104 gives instructions for cooking beef brisket. However, these are not meats that I would recommend you try to cook if you have absolutely no cooking experience.

Chicken thighs can be as little as £3.38 per Kg, or, if you buy them frozen, £2.00 per Kg. This would give you approximately 12 chicken thighs.

Chicken drumsticks are approximately £2.47 per Kg. Approximately 12 drumsticks.

However, bear in mind that when you buy this meat, you are also paying for the weight of the bone, that you do not eat. Thighs and drumsticks will take a little while to cook thoroughly and be tender.

One **chicken breast** costs approximately £1.50. You can make it stretch between two meals, if you add extras veggies to the recipe. It is also very quick and easy to cook.

For example, you could cook Creamy Chicken from "Nosh 4 Students", see opposite, and add extra mushrooms.

Minced lamb and beef are around £3.00 per Kg. You would use approximately 125g per person for a meal. This is good value, as it is all meat and very versatile and quick to use.

Creamy Chicken

- **rice** to serve
- **pilau rice seasoning**

- 1 teaspoon **butter**
- ½ **onion**, chopped
- 1 **chicken breast**, cut into pieces
- 1 clove **garlic**, finely chopped
- 2 - 3 **mushrooms**, sliced
- ¼ pint **double cream**
- 1 **chicken stock cube**, crumbled
- ½ teaspoon freeze dried **basil**

1. Put rice on to cook with ½ teaspoon pilau seasoning (see page 86).
2. Fry onions in the butter until soft.
3. Add the chicken breast and the garlic. Cook on a high heat until the chicken is no longer pink. Add the mushrooms and cook for 2 minutes.
4. Add the cream and stock cube. Cook gently for 5 - 10 minutes, stirring occasionally.
5. Add the basil and cook for one minute.
6. Serve with rice.

Question 10

Getting the balance between inexpensive and good, nutritional food is not easy, Alex. **Pulses**, especially if you buy them dried and soak them, are very cheap and are also high in protein, vitamins and minerals, making them an excellent food. In order to enjoy pulses, you need to find good recipes to make them appetizing and tasty. I have a few in "Vegetarian Nosh 4 Students". Pulses include chickpeas, black eyed beans, borlotti beans, broad beans, butter beans, cannellini beans, kidney beans, lentils and pinto beans. There is a recipe using chickpeas on page 22.

Mince is one of the cheapest meats to buy. Don't be fooled into buying really cheap mince, as it can be full of fat and not so tasty.

Chicken thighs are also good value and inexpensive. You will need to find some good recipes, for example Chicken Hot Pot on page 147. Be aware that they need a little bit longer to cook, in order for them to be tender.

Eggs are relatively cheap, but need to be part of a balanced diet. They are also quite versatile, for instance, omelettes, poached eggs, fried eggs, frittatas etc.

Cheese has a good balance of fat, protein and carbohydrate and is not too expensive. Note, however, that just eating cheese does not provide you with a well balanced diet.

Chickpea Patties

Serves 2

- 400g tin of **chickpeas**, rinsed and drained
- ½ **onion**, grated
- 1 slice of **wholemeal bread**, left to go a bit dry, then crumbled
- 1 **egg**, beaten
- small **courgette**, grated
- 1 teaspoon **chives**
- **oil** to fry

Yogurt dressing

- 3 tablespoons **natural yogurt**
- 1 tablespoon **mango** or **fruit chutney**
- 1 teaspoon **mint**

Spicy onions

- 1 tablespoon **oil**
- 1 large **onion**, sliced
- 1 teaspoon **curry paste**

1. Mash the drained chickpeas with a fork. It does not matter if there are a few whole ones in there.
2. Squeeze out the moisture from the grated onion. Mix together in a bowl with the courgette and chick peas.
3. Mix the egg and crumbled bread together in a separate bowl. Mix with the rest of the patty ingredients. The mixture should be fairly stiff. Tip out onto a surface and, with floured hands (if you have any flour), form 4 patties.
4. Heat the oil in a frying pan and put the patties in to fry. Keep the heat moderate and cook for about 5 minutes each side.
5. While they are cooking make the yogurt dressing. Simply mix the ingredients together.
6. To make the spicy onions, fry the sliced onions in a saucepan on a fairly high heat. Allow them to brown, then add the curry paste and mix well. Cook for 1 minute and then take off the heat.

1

2

3

Chickpeas

3a

4

5 minutes
each side

Question 11

> ## "What is the best white fish to buy on a budget as opposed to cod?" *A Merrick*

Fish is an important foodstuff. It is a good source of vitamins and minerals. Oily fish, such as salmon, mackerel, sardines and trout are rich in omega 3 fatty acids (good for you).

Here are some approximate price ideas for the cheaper types of fish:

Fresh fish

Mackerel per person - £1.20

Trout fillets per person - £1.50

Haddock fillets per person - £1.55

Pollock fillets per person - £1.20

One of the best buys is a pack of fish pie mix for £3.00 which would serve 2 - 3 people.

Opposite is a recipe for fish pie.

Frozen fish

Frozen fish is quite a bit cheaper, you just need to give it time to defrost.

Cod steaks are 50p each, although quite small

Coley steaks are 47p each, although also quite small

Haddock steak are £1.00 each

Best buy would be a 520g pack of white fish fillets for £1.94. Also great for fish pie. Take as much as you need out of the pack and return the rest to the freezer.

Fisherman's Pie

Serves 2

Preparation time 20 minutes, cooking time 20 minutes

- 1 mug **milk**
- 2 pieces **cod or haddock fillet** (defrost if frozen)
- 2 teaspoons **cornflour**
- **salt** and **pepper**
- 2 hard-boiled **eggs**, each cut into 4 (see page 94)
- 1 teaspoon freeze-dried **parsley or basil**
- 5 medium **potatoes**, washed and diced
- 1 teaspoon **butter**
- ½ mug grated **cheese**

+ 1 teaspoon cornflour
+ a little milk

1. Preheat the oven to 200°C fan oven/220°C/Gas 7.
2. Place the milk and fish in the frying pan and simmer gently for approximately 5 minutes, or until the fish turns white.
3. Mix the cornflour with a little milk to make a paste and add to the pan. Stir well into the milk. The sauce will thicken. Season with salt and pepper and gently break up the fish.
4. Add the hard-boiled egg and the herbs. Mix gently and pour into a casserole dish.
5. Boil the diced potatoes for 8 - 10 minutes, drain off the water, add the butter and stir gently.
6. Place the potatoes on the top of the fish mixture and top with the grated cheese.
7. Cook for 20 minutes, until the top is browned.
8. Serve with green vegetables or salad.

Shopping

Question 12

"What is the best supermarket?"

Sam MacMaws

"What supermarket is best for a student to shop at?"

Sanchit Kapoo

There are lots of things to bear in mind when shopping. **The cheapest supermarket is not necessarily the best.** The supermarkets compete on the TV to tell you which one is the cheapest. I always think that we generally get what we pay for, so just buying cheap is not always the best.

For a student, **convenience is a huge factor**. I am thinking that the majority of you will not have access to a car. The cheapest supermarket may require that you get a taxi back to your home with the shopping. This added expense makes it no longer the cheapest supermarket.

I would choose a supermarket which sells good, fresh produce. This would include one that sells fresh meat, vegetables and fruit. Go there on a regular basis. However, I would recommend that, perhaps once a month, you go to the cheaper supermarket and buy in bulk the things that do not need to be fresh. This includes tinned and frozen foods, plus cleaning and washing things.

If your parents **shop at places like Costco or Makro**, which are big wholesale stores, go home when Mum is shopping there. You can get tinned foods for amazing prices compared with normal supermarkets. Things like mince and chicken can be bought in bulk and separated into smaller quantities and frozen. You will, of course, need some cooperation from Mum or Dad on this idea!

Shopping wisely is as good as shopping cheaply. When you see things on special offer in the supermarket, chicken thighs or breast, buy them and put them in the freezer. You may need to separate them into portions before freezing.

ALDI ? Londis TESCO ? Co-op ?
? COSTCO ? ? LIDL Costcutter ? ?
Happy Shopper ? ?
? Sainsbury's ? Iceland ? MAKRO ?
M&S ? ASDA ? Morrisons ? Waitrose

Question 13

> ## "What are 10 essential ingredients for a student cupboard?"
> *Jodie Brumhead*

As a student, either in halls or in shared accommodation, you need to be selective when buying and get the things you need and want to use.

Storecupboard ingredients that will be very useful:

- sugar
- flour
- oil to cook with
- salt and pepper
- stock cubes
- tomato purée
- rice
- pasta
- cereal
- 1 packet of long life milk

> ## "What are good condiments/ingredients to keep in your storecupboard?"
> *Lucy McColm*

Storecupboard as above, plus

- tinned chopped tomatoes
- tin of baked beans
- tomato sauce
- HP sauce
- soy sauce
- curry paste
- tea
- coffee

Fridge

- butter/spread
- milk
- eggs
- cheese
- mayo

Useful Herbs and spices:

- mixed dried herbs
- dried basil
- chilli flakes
- paprika

28 shopping

Question 14

"For an average student are there any cheaper alternatives to the expensive spices on the shop shelves?" *Anthony Blyth*

Yes there are, Anthony. You can buy larger packets of many spices from supermarkets and from Asian supermarkets. You will need to keep them in sealed jars once you have opened the packets. Just save up some jam jars, make sure that their lids are not rusty.

Mixed spices for a curry or separate?

Apurva Chitnis

If you have the time to cook with separate spices and cook them together before making the curry, this is always best and really satisfying. You will get a great meal at the end of your efforts. However, for students who have limited time and space in the kitchen, I would recommend Pataks curry pastes. They have already mixed the spices for you. I would not recommend just using curry powder on its own.

Freezing & Defrosting

Question 15

Things that don't freeze

Most fruits don't freeze too well. The ones you buy in the supermarkets have been specially frozen, i.e. laid out and frozen individually. Even these come out a bit mushy.

Don't Freeze

- most green or leafy vegetables
- salad stuff, tomatoes, cucumbers, etc.
- blocks of cheese. They lose their flavour if you freeze them, although, dishes containing cooked cheese are usually OK.
- cream (It does not freeze well.)

Good things for students to think of freezing

As a student, there are many meals where you can cook enough for 2 or 3 and then freeze the portions you don't eat. For example, if you make Spaghetti Bolognese or soups, eat some and freeze the rest. Always make sure the food is completely cool before you put it in the freezer.

Milk is OK in plastic bottles, not glass bottles, and is good as a stand by.

If you see bargain packs of meat in the supermarket, buy them and divide into smaller portions. Put them in freezer bags and freeze for a later day.

"Freezing food - what can you freeze and eat later?"
Dan Richter

With most meals, you can make enough for two people and freeze one half to eat later. Things that don't reheat well are meals containing eggs and shellfish. Spag Bol, Chilli, Shepherd's Pie, stews and soups are great when reheated.

Can you refreeze meat once it has been defrosted?
Abigail Wilson

NO!

"I'm a big fried breakfast fan but forget to buy eggs. I was wondering if I can freeze eggs and, if so, how should I unfreeze them?"
Esther Gore

You can freeze eggs, but it is a bit of a bother. You cannot freeze them whole. You need to crack the egg, beat it until smooth. Pour into silicon muffin holders and put in the freezer. Once they are frozen, pop them out into sealed freezer bags and keep in the freezer until you need them.

Obviously, you will only be able to do scrambled eggs or omellettes.

To defrost, leave in the fridge overnight.

BRRRR!!!

Question 16

"How do you defrost stuff when it comes to it?"
Dan Richter

We need to take great care when defrosting food. If we just take it out of the fridge and leave it at room temperature, the outside of the food defrosts a long time before the inside, thereby leaving parts of the food vulnerable at room temperature.

If you can, it is best to cut up the food you want to defrost.

Here are three ways to safely defrost food:

1. The easiest way is to take the food out of the freezer the night before and leave it all night in the fridge.

2. If you are in more of a hurry, then put the food in a plastic bag or the covering it has been frozen in. Place in a large bowl of cold water. Change this water every hour or so, until the food is defrosted.

3. Defrost in the microwave on a defrost setting. I would not recommend this for whole chickens or larger pieces of meat, as the outside of the food begins to cook in the microwave. For the same reason, if you do defrost in the microwave, cook the food immediately.

Food
Hygiene

Food poisoning?

You may find the idea of getting food poisoning reasonably attractive, as you can legitimately take a few days off Uni. Maybe you would get a little more attention from your girlfriend/boyfriend. The reality is so different. You definitely need to stay near a toilet. Most of the time you don't know whether you need the loo or the sink or both! Your head will be banging so much, you may not recognize your girlfriend/boyfriend. It can also be very painful. **YOU NEED TO AVOID THIS.**

Here are some, hopefully, useful ways to avoid the 'lurgi' or even just painful gut experiences.

Cling film is a great invention. If you use it, it will keep your food from becoming contaminated by anything disgusting your housemates might leave in the fridge. It also keeps things from drying up and is useful when reheating food in the microwave. Take care that you buy the type which is safe to use in the microwave.

Remember, when you have opened a can of food, don't put the can in the fridge. Decant into a bowl and cover with cling film.

Question 17

"We always got told never to reheat rice: Is that just an urban myth?" *Dan Richter*

"Is it safe to reheat rice and chicken?" *Bethany Simpkin*

It is not the re-heating that is the problem, but how you have dealt with the rice before re-heating. The Bacillus cereus spores that can be present in uncooked rice can survive the cooking process. If it is then left to stand at room temperature, the spores will germinate into bacteria and will produce toxins which can cause unwanted gut experiences. Re-heating will not kill this bacteria.

Rice needs to be cooled as quickly as possible. Any leftovers you have should be transferred to a clean bowl, ready to put in the fridge. Put in the fridge as soon as it is cooled.

Don't reheat after the first day.

> "Can you reheat chicken? If so how do you do it safely?"
> *Elliot Hodges*

> "What's the best way to reheat food safely?"
> *Matt Harrison*

Yes, you can reheat chicken. Again, the main thing to be careful with is not to leave the chicken at room temperature after is has cooled, but to put it in the fridge immediately.

You also need to reheat the cooked chicken thoroughly. Different food agencies describe this as 'piping hot'.

Put the food to be re-heated on a plate and cover with cling film. Heat for 3½ - 4 minutes on maximum heat. When you take off the cling film, the food should be steaming and the plate too hot for you to handle. This would be a good indication of 'piping hot'.

> "How long does boiled rice last before you can fry it?"
> *Adrian Thornton*

If you cook rice to eat with a meal one day, you can fry it the next day. When you fry rice it is the same as re-heating, so be careful to heat to a piping hot temperature.

food hygiene 37

The same rules apply to all foods. Cool them as quickly as possible and put them in the fridge. Only heat things up the next day. After that, throw away the cooked food.

A few things I would not reheat are shellfish, any kind of bought burger, peas because they usually explode and eggs because they will go very rubbery.

Microwaving food usually makes it tough or rubbery. The better thing to do is **share your food with a flat mate** when it is freshly cooked and hope that they will do the same for you.

Make sure that **your microwave is in good order.** Old machines can be dangerous and do not reheat food properly.

Question 18

"What happens if you eat food that has green bits on it/potatoes with ears?"

Dan Richter

It's best not to eat potatoes when they have gone green and sprouted ears. When they look like this, they will contain high levels of toxins called glycoalkaloids (a family of plant poisons!). These could give you sickness and diarrhoea. Something I am sure you would like to avoid.

If the potato just has a small amount of green on it or a small 'ear', just cut them off, along with a good bit of the surrounding area. If it's green all over and has more than a couple of 'ears', please throw it away.

You can also help your potatoes not to develop these nasty things by keeping them in a cool, dark place. They do not need to be in the fridge, but covered and away from the light.

Question 19

"Storing food - I know it sounds silly, but cupboard/fridge where do I put it all?"

Dan Richter

Fridge

Keep everything covered. Cling film is a great friend. Never put opened tins in the fridge. Transfer the contents to a bowl and cover with cling film. Plastic, squeezy pegs are also great for keeping packets closed in the cupboards and in the freezer. Always keep the following in the fridge:

- milk,
- butter/spread
- eggs
- cheese
- cream
- yogurt
- anything in an opened jar (read labels for how long you can keep it, even in the fridge)
- salad
- veg, (apart from potatoes, they need to be in a cool, dark place.)
- mayo
- fruit, apples, pears, peaches
- fruit juice
- liquid stock (small bottles)

Cupboards

- unopened tins
- flour, keep sealed
- sugar, keep sealed
- spices, keep sealed
- herbs
- tomato purée
- stock cubes
- cooking oil
- rice
- pasta
- dried fruit
- cereal

Out of fridge or cupboard

- Bananas cause other fruit to ripen quickly, so keep them separate.

COOL, DARK
PLACE

Question 20

"How do I know when food is really past it? For instance, when can I get away with eating meat that is a few days past the sell-by date, how can I tell if it's still safe and should I ever risk it? Also, if I purchased meat and kept it in the fridge, could I freeze it on the day it goes out of date and use it weeks later?" *Joel Bennett*

I would say food needs to be cooked no later than one day after the 'sell-by' date. I would also say, generally, if in doubt, bin it. Don't risk anything, unless you want to sample some food poisoning. If you have some meat that is several days past its sell-by date, I think you will smell that it is not fit to eat.

If you purchase some fresh meat, you need to cook it, or freeze it, that day, or the day after. If you cook it, you can put a portion of what you cook in the freezer, or the fridge, to eat the next day. Make sure that it is completely cooled before you put it in either the fridge or freezer. Rather than freeze meat that is going out of date, I would cook it and then freeze it. Defrosting 'going out of date meat' is not a good idea.

Food does not always 'look' past it, even when it is. Fresh red meat will look nice and pink or red, whereas, when it gets a bit older, it begins to look more brown or khaki coloured. It may have a stronger or strange smell. Potatoes, see page 39, give themselves away. If you have vegetables that should be crisp, but have gone a bit soft, they will not do you a lot of good. If you have vegetables that should be green and now look browny yellow, throw them away.

Generally, if things have a strange smell, or look pretty 'ropy', I would not eat them.

Question 21

"What is the best way to make raw materials last?" *Matt Harrison*

Shop wisely, plan what you are going to eat and buy only enough for what you need.

Cling film and zip lock poly bags are great friends. Keep things covered in the fridge, as it keeps the food fresher and stops it drying up around the edges. It also prevents cross-contamination from other foods, which may have been inadvertently left in there.

Meat - freeze it, or cook it and freeze it. If you buy fresh meat from the supermarket and want to freeze it, simply divide into smaller portions and place in freezer bags.

Vegetables and fruit - keep covered in the fridge. Bananas are best out of the fridge and separate from other fruits. If you but bananas in a bowl of fruit, they will speed up the ripening process of the other fruits.

Potatoes and **onions** should be kept in a cool dark place, as the light makes potatoes go green quicker.

If you buy **celery**, it is best to cut off the root at the bottom, put the celery in a glass of water and put in the fridge.

Salads are best in the salad drawer at the bottom of the fridge. If you are sharing a fridge, you may not have this luxury, so keep the salads in a plastic box.

Milk, cheese and eggs need to be in the fridge. Eggs are best kept in their original containers. Cheese needs to be kept covered or it will go dry. Cling film is great.

Keep **opened jars** in the fridge. Read the label to check how long it will last.

Bread is best kept out of the fridge and in its wrapper. Keep the bag closed, with as little air in it as possible. If you buy a large loaf, freeze half of it. If you buy fresh, white, crusty loaves from the supermarket bakery, they will tend to become very dry by the next day. If you really like this kind of bread, you will need to buy smaller loaves, or share them with your housemates.

Jams are best kept in the fridge once opened.

Question 22

"How long can garlic be kept till it goes off?"
Jack Josse

Garlic will keep for quite a while, either in a garlic pot (a ceramic pot with air holes in it) or in the fridge. When you cut it open and the middles are green, it will not taste too good. If the garlic has begun to dry out and go soft, this is also an indication that it has lost its freshness and will not be too good.

"How long does fresh cream take till it goes off?"
Jordan Sharp

Fresh cream usually has a sell-by and use-by date on it. Left unopened, it will keep a few days. Once opened, stick to the use-by date. If you smell the cream and it smells like cheese, then it has 'gone off'. Once you have opened the cream, make sure the pot is resealed, as it will take on any other smells in your fridge.

"How long after the expiry date can I eat yogurt without being sick?"
Jordan Sharp

Some people say that you can eat yogurt up to one week after the expiration date, if the carton has not been opened. Personally, I would not take the chance. After the expiration date, the top on the yogurt starts to puff up into a dome. This tells me that something is fermenting in there and I would not want to eat it.

Question 23

> "If you leave leftover meat in the fridge how long till it is unsafe to eat? *Robert Masson*

If the meat is cooked, it is safe to eat the next day, but not after that.

Raw meat needs to be cooked the day it is bought, or the day after.

> "What is the longest time I can store a meal after it has been cooked?"
> *Charlotte Ironside*

If it has been put in the fridge as soon as it has cooled, then it can be eaten the next day, but not after that. It should be thoroughly reheated, until it is piping hot, see page 37.

Many cooked meals are OK eaten the next day, if they contain chicken or red meats. Be careful to reheat food thoroughly. A plate of food takes approximately 3½ minutes on full power in a microwave to be heated right through. Always check the centre of the plate, as the microwave works from the outside in.

Shellfish should never be reheated, but always eaten straight away.

> "How long does chicken stock last in the fridge?"
> *Adrain Thornton*

If you have fresh chicken stock, it is the same as a chicken. If you have gone to the bother of making fresh stock, freeze any that you don't use the day you make it. Jars of concentrated liquid chicken stock will have a use-by date after opening. Read the relevant instructions.

Question 24

> "Can you reheat Chinese takeaway the morning after you have eaten it?"
>
> *Henry Waine*

> "How long can I keep leftover takeaway in the fridge?"
>
> *Josh Chiswell*

Takeaways are expensive and so not to be wasted. If you put it in the fridge as soon as it has cooled, and kept it covered, it should be OK to reheat and eat the next day, but not the day after.

Takeaway often includes rice. The same for reheating rules would apply, see page 36. If you have left it open in the kitchen all evening, have come to clear up at 2.00 in the morning and then put it in the fridge, I would say don't eat it. If in doubt, don't eat.

I would never reheat takeaway burgers, whole chickens or kebabs.

For reheating food see page 37. Remember, food should always be reheated until it is 'piping hot'.

Question 25

> "How long will things last in the cupboard, in jars etc. eg. curry paste?"
>
> *Rob Gainer*

Jars and tins will have a use-by date on them. This is usually quite a long time after purchase.

Once you have opened a jar, keep it in the fridge and stick with the instructions on the pack. Some things will only last a couple of days once opened, others, like curry pastes and mayo, will last longer. The labels on the jars and tins give an accurate guide.

Once you have opened a tin and used part of it, you need to decant the remaining food into a bowl and cover with cling film and put in the fridge. Again, look at the label to see how long it will last.

Telltale signs for everything are mould and bad smells. Once things have gone this far, do not be tempted to just spoon off the mouldy bit and eat the rest.

Question 26

"If you have bought 'reduced to clear' chicken, so it goes out of date on that day and then you freeze it, and then you cook it again, do you have to eat it on the day you have cooked it or is it OK to keep for another day to reheat at a later point?"

Thomas Povey

Buying the 'reduced to clear' chicken is a great idea. But if you freeze it, as it defrosts, it is in danger of going out of date. Not too safe.

I would be more inclined to cook the chicken on the day you buy it. Eat whatever you want that day. The cooked meat will be OK for the next day, or you can freeze it to use cold in sandwiches etc. another day.

Be careful when defrosting chicken. The best way is to leave it in the fridge overnight. Leaving it out on a work surface means that the outside of the chicken, which defrosts first, is at room temperature for quite a while.

Question 27

> "Is it true that 'slightly off' cheese is better for cooking, as it has a stronger flavour, as, for example, when Italians use the mouldy rind of parmesan?"
>
> *Adrian Thornton*

No, it's not.

I am not aware that Italians use the mouldy bit of the parmesan. Parmesan takes a couple of years to mature, but still needs to be well looked after. If you keep it in the fridge and wrapped in a sealed bag it will keep for ages. Cut off any mould before you use it.

Some cheeses, like Roquefort, Gorgonzola and Blue Brie are made with harmless moulds and are perfectly safe to eat. Normal cheeses, like Cheddar, Cheshire etc., are not meant to be mouldy. They have different levels of 'maturity' - the more mature, the stronger the flavour. (That's why grandads are often quite interesting!) The mould that may grow on cheese is not part of a controlled manufacturing process and can contain harmful bacteria such as salmonella and E.coli. If there is a little bit of mould on some cheese, you can just cut it off and eat the rest. If the mould has spread more over the cheese, then throw it away.

Soft cheeses, or any cheese that has been purchased shredded or sliced that develop mould, need to be thrown away.

Storing cheese in the fridge and making sure that it is in a sealed box, or covered in cling film, will help to prevent mould. It will also stop any mould which does grow contaminating other food stuff in the fridge.

Good Fridge

Bad Fridge

Question 28

"Sometimes fish or meat gives off a weird smell if left in your freezer. How can I prevent that?"

Enosh Bashir Sira

When you freeze fish, if you pick it up and smell it, it will smell 'fishy' and that is OK. It should not make the whole freezer smell. If it does do this throw it away. If, when you open the freezer, there is a terrible smell, you need to locate the source and throw it away.

Only freeze things that are fresh. Meat and fish should be frozen on the day it is purchased. Always put in freezer bags. Not all poly bags are suitable for freezing.

As a student, you will share a freezer and, at best, have a freezer drawer to yourself. You need to use this wisely. Use the freezer to keep meals when you have made enough for two and you are on your own. It's also useful to freeze bargain meats purchased from the supermarket.

Healthy Eating

Question 29

"Is frozen veg as good for me as fresh veg?"
Hannah Rycraft

It is good that you are talking about veg. Any veg is better than none. I would always go for fresh veg and fruit, but we need to make sure that it is fresh. Buying from the general store round the corner may not give us fresh stuff. Buying from a farm shop should give good fresh veg, as will a good supermarket. We need to buy carefully. Don't buy too much at once and then leave it in the fridge for a week. The poor veg will have lost a bit of its nutrition by then.

Having said this, frozen veg is not bad for us. Generally, it has been taken straight from the farm to the freezer people and should be high in nutrients. The same applies to some tinned produce. Choose things with no added salt, sugar, colouring or preservatives and you will be OK. Tinned vegetables can lose some of their nutrients during the canning process. Tinned pulses are fine, but again watch for any additives and make sure you rinse them well.

We also need to be careful how we cook vegetables and not over cook them. A little 'al dente' (crisp and crunchy) is good. If vegetables are boiled fast, or for a long time, and then cooked until they are soggy, most of the nutrients will be destroyed.

Question 30

"What is the healthiest way of making chips?"
Annabel Walker

"Are there healthier ways to cook things like burgers and chips?"
Laura Dawson

Yes. Use the right kind of cooking oil, one low in saturated fats and high in monounsaturated fats. These would be sunflower oil, olive oil, canola oil or corn oil. Don't deep-fry chips.

Use as little oil as possible. The best way to do this is to cook the chips in the oven like potato wedges.

Chips/Potato Wedges the healthy way

1. Preheat the oven to 180°C fan oven/200°C/Gas 6.
2. Wash the potatoes and cut them into long wedges.
3. Put a little oil on a baking tray and mix it into the wedges with your fingers, so that each one has a thin coat. Try to stand all the wedges on their 'backs'; that way more of the wedge will brown. Season with salt and pepper.
4. Place in the oven for 25 - 30 minutes. They should be browned by then.

Yummy/Healthy Burgers

Don't just buy them from the supermarket.

Makes 2

Preparation time 20 minutes, cooking time 20 minutes

- 250g pack of lean **mince**
- 1 **egg**, beaten
- **oil** to fry
- 2 flat **bread buns**
- any combination of **lettuce**, **tomatoes**, **cucumber**, **gherkin** etc.
- **mayo**, **tomato sauce** or **mustard**

1. Mix the mince and the egg together. Season well with salt and pepper.
2. Divide the mixture into 2 and shape the burgers with your hands so they are about 1" thick.
3. Heat a small amount of oil in a frying pan. When hot, add the burgers. Cook for 4 - 5 minutes then carefully turn them over. Cook for a further 4 - 5 minutes.
4. Using a fork, check to see that the inside of the burger is cooked, i.e. that the meat is no longer pink. If not, turn down the heat and cook a little bit longer, turning the burgers.
5. Put the cooked burger into the bread bun. Add salad and the sauces to your taste.

Question 31

> "What's the best thing to eat at breakfast that will last a long time, i.e. so I don't get hungry?"
>
> *Alison Tang*
>
> "What is the healthiest breakfast, and should I have it all the time for breakfast?"
>
> *Charlie Weatherill*

Breakfast is an important meal and should not be skipped. Eating a good breakfast sets you up for the rest of the day. If you miss breakfast, you will become tired very early in the day. If you just depend on things like Mars Bars, Red Bull and coffee to give you an energy boost, this will only be temporary. You will get a boost of energy for a short time, and then go low. If you have another, there will be another short boost of energy but then you will go even lower, and so on. Eventually you will feel a bit wrecked.

Here are a few healthy suggestions. Don't eat the same thing every day, you will just get bored with it.

1. A bowl of **good cereal** containing grains and fruit or nuts. Jordans do a good, tasty range of breakfast cereals. Use with semi skimmed milk. Take a piece of fruit as you dash out of the house.
2. A **fruit smoothie**. If you have a hand-held blender (recommended), put a banana, a couple of tablespoons of yogurt, a teaspoon of honey and some skimmed milk in a jug and whizz it up. Maybe have with a piece of toast. Very quick and very nutritious.
3. **Fruit and yogurt**. Put a pot of natural or good fruit yogurt in a bowl. Top with some honey, chopped fruit and muesli.
4. A **scrambled egg sandwich**. Scramble two eggs, see page 95. Put between two slices of wholemeal bread. Add salt and pepper. Enjoy with a glass of fruit juice.

Here are a few **energy giving foods** (some are included in the breakfasts suggested above):

Whole grains are high in fibre and can slow down the absorption of some carbohydrates.

Oatmeal, good source of fibre.

Bananas are packed with potassium, you see tennis players eating them between sets.

Orange juice is high in vitamin C.

Beans, not so much baked beans, are high in proteins, fibre, minerals and vitamins.

Dried fruits, such as apricots, figs and raisins, are great to eat as snacks.

Yogurt gives energy and is easy to carry around as a snack.

AT 8.00 a.m. THE TORTOISE HAD A GOOD BREAKFAST

AT 8.45 a.m. THE HARE HAD A RED BULL & A COFFEE

AROUND 11.30 a.m. THE HARE FELT QUITE LOW

AT 11.30 a.m. THE TORTOISE MARCHED STEADILY TO LUNCH

Question 32

"To Quorn or not to Quorn?" *Apurvas Chitnis*

There is debate as to the safety of Quorn, because it is made from a fungus and can cause allergic reactions in some people. However, the Food Standards Agency has looked at all the evidence and believes that Quorn is safe to eat. Other foods, dairy, shellfish and peanuts, can also cause allergies, but the risk from Quorn seems to be low.

Quorn is rich in protein and is now made into 'convenience foods', which you can buy from the freezer sections in the supermarket. It does not have a great advantage for non vegetarians, as it is not particularly cheap.

Quorn does not have a lot of taste in itself, so needs to be included in a tasty recipe. The Quorn mince is good and can be used in things like Spaghetti Bolognese or Chilli.

Question 33

"Is white meat better than red?"

Deborah Uwayo

"What's the healthier meat to eat?"

Jonathan Briscoe

"What is better, red or white meat?"

Jobie Warner

I don't think it's a question of red or white meat, but rather the fat content of either. Lean red meat contains 4.8g of fat per 100g, whereas, lean white poultry meat contains 1.3g of fat per 100g. The darker poultry meat contains more fat. Lean red and white meat are both healthy. The important thing is to remove the sources of fat before cooking. For instance, the skin and fat from chicken breasts or thighs and any fat from red meat.

If you are concerned about healthy meat, be careful when buying mince. Usually all the fat will be minced into what you buy, so you will need to buy lean beef, pork or lamb mince. You will see this when you cook cheaper mince - the fat floats to the top and you need to scoop it off. Remember you have paid for that fat!

Question 34

"Are there any cheap but healthy desserts that you would recommend for students?"

Anthony Blyth

Not sure many desserts are completely healthy, but here are a couple to try and they are not too expensive.

Baked Apples

Serves 1

Serve with a little yogurt. If you want to be a little less healthy, you can buy some ready-made custard.

- 1 large **cooking apple**
- 1 tablespoon **brown sugar**
- 2 tablespoons **sultanas** or **raisins**
- a little **butter**
- 1 dessertspoon **honey**
- 1 tablespoon **water**

1. Preheat the oven to 180°C fan oven/200°C/Gas 6.
2. Wash the apple and cut out the core from the centre, leaving the apple whole. Score a horizontal line around the centre of the apple. This stops the skin from bursting.
3. Mix together the sugar and the fruit. Stuff it into the space where the core was. Place on an ovenproof dish; a casserole dish is fine. Place small pieces of butter around the top of the apple. Spoon the honey and then the water over the apple. If you have spare fruit and sugar, sprinkle around the bottom of the apple. It will turn into toffee as the apple cooks.
4. Bake in the oven for 25-30 minutes.

Fruit Salad   Serves 2 - 3

Fruit salad will not last more than one day, as the fruits will begin to go brown. If you just have two or three fruits, you can liven them up by making them into a salad. You can use a variety of fruits, which could include those listed below:

- apples
- pears
- oranges
- bananas
- seedless grapes
- strawberries
- kiwi fruits
- pineapple
- peaches
- nectarines
- raspberries

For the juice

- You can use either pure **apple** or **orange fruit juice**.
- If you prefer a more tangy fruit salad, try the following:
- 1 **lemon**
- 1 **orange**
- 1 tablespoon **sugar**
- ¼ mug **water**

1. To make the juice, grate the rind of the lemon and the orange and squeeze the juices from both fruits. Add the sugar and the water. Leave for the sugar to dissolve.
2. Cut the fruit into small pieces and mix together. If you use raspberries and strawberries, add them at the end, or they will break up in the mix and everything will be pink!
3. Serve with yogurt.

Question 35

> "Which type of bread do you recommend?"
> *Jake Humphrey*
>
> "Is there much difference between white and brown bread?"
> *Todd Rayner*
>
> "Does brown bread taste nicer than white?"
> *Jonathan Briscoe*

I would recommend good 'brown' bread, the stuff with nothing taken out, not just the stuff that looks brown. Bread which states it is 'whole-wheat' or 'wholemeal' is what you need to look for.

The taste of good brown bread is much better than white. Once you are used to eating brown bread and then go back to white, you will find that the white bread has very little taste and has little or no texture. There are good reasons for this.

I could just say "brown bread is much better for you", but if you are used to white bread, that is not a good enough reason. White bread is made from flour from which the bran and wheat germ have been removed. In other words, most of the healthy nutrients have been taken out. White bread is lower in zinc, fibre, thiamin and niacin. Once the bran and germ have been removed, the flour is then bleached with potassium bromate, benzoyl peroxide or chlorine dioxide gas. Still wanting to eat white bread?????

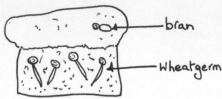

Question 36

"If you were at Uni, would you suggest using tinned fruit, because it's often said to be more unhealthy, but it lasts longer?"

Beth Mulchinock

From a taste, looks and texture point of view, fresh fruit would win every time. It is easier to carry a banana or an apple than it is a tin of fruit. However, good tinned fruit can have almost the same nutritional value. It is canned very soon after picking, whereas fresh fruit sometimes has to travel quite a long way. We need to be careful not to keep fresh fruit out in a bowl for long periods of time, as it will deteriorate. Often, fruit has gone bad before we have had the time to eat it; this is a waste of money.

Some things to consider when buying canned fruit:

If the fruit has been peeled, it will have lost some of its fibre content.

Vitamin C is sensitive to the heat process involved in canning fruit and can sometimes be destroyed. Vitamins A & B and potassium stay intact.

Look for fruit packed in its own juice, or in water, not in sugary syrup.

There is a range of 'Nature's Finest', fruit packed in its own juice. They have no added sugar, preservatives, added colour or added flavour.

Frozen fruit is very useful for things like smoothies. If you keep a pack of summer fruits in the freezer, just take a few out, whizz together with some yogurt and apple juice and you will have a healthy smoothie.

Dried fruit will lose some of its vitamin C during the drying process, but is still rich in fibre and potassium. They are very easy to carry around as a snack.

Question 37

> "What are the healthiest ways of cooking different foods, e.g. steaming veg?"
>
> *Pippa Nelson*

If you want to retain all the vitamins and minerals in any kind of food, there are several things to bear in mind:

1. Cook and eat the food as soon as possible after purchase. The longer you store it, the more nutrients will be destroyed.
2. Cook vegetables in a minimal amount of water, i.e. just enough to cover them.
3. Don't cook food for longer than necessary. Vegetables are better a bit crunchy than soggy.
4. Boiling food gently, not boiling on a high heat, preserves more nutrients.
5. Cut up vegetables just before cooking. Don't cut them up and leave them around for a long time before cooking.

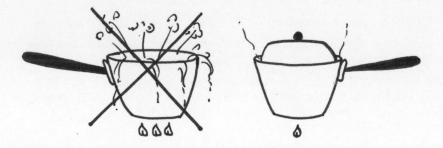

Steaming or poaching are good methods of cooking. If you are vegetarian, buying a steamer, even as a student, could be a good idea. However, boiling in a small amount of water is almost as good.

Poaching is a good, gentle method of cooking eggs, fish and chicken. To poach eggs see page 93.

To poach chicken breast

1. Put the chicken breast in a saucepan, with enough boiling water to cover it. Season well and bring to the boil.
2. Take off the heat and leave to stand, with the lid on, for 15 minutes.

bring to the boil

leave for 15 mins

To poach fish

1. Put a little boiling water in a frying pan.
2. Add the fish, season well, and bring to the boil. Turn down to simmer and place a lid over the fish.
3. Allow to simmer for 5 - 10 minutes, depending on the thickness of the fish. The fish will go white and flake away from the skin when it is cooked.

5-10 mins

Question 38

"If it's greasy, is it bad for you?" *Kyle Daniel*

"Is there any substitute for oil or butter, i.e. a low fat option?" *Beth Mulchinock*

Consuming excessive amounts of the wrong type of fat is not healthy. However, our bodies need small amounts of fat to work properly. We need to eat much less saturated fats.

Saturated fats, the bad ones, are found in butter, lard, ghee, fatty meats (found in sausages and pies), full-fat milk, cream, crème fraîche, ice cream, hard cheese, crisps, coconut oil, biscuits, cakes and pastries, sweets and chocolate. In other words all the things we like!

We can still eat some of these things, but less of them and not all of them. Choose lean meats and skinless poultry and cut off any fat before you cook it. You can grill or oven-cook meat instead of frying it. Eat less pastry and cakes.

Choose foods with lower levels of saturated fats. Cook with unsaturated vegetables oils, such as sunflower oil or olive oil. Look for low fat milk and yogurt. Use olive oil spreads, instead of butter.

"What is the best type of oil to cook with?"

John Norrie

So long as you are careful not to use too much fat in your cooking, the following oils will be OK. They are low in saturated fats and some have a high concentration of monounsaturated fats - olive oil, for instance.

- canola oil
- peanut oil
- olive oil
- non-hydrogenated soft margarine
- sunflower oil

The following fats are high in saturated fats and not to be recommended for use on a regular basis:

- lard type oils
- hard margarine
- butter
- coconut oil
- ghee

For general frying, stir frying etc. use sunflower oil.

For roasting potatoes you can use olive oil.

For salad dressings use olive oil.

When cooking pancakes it is best to use a lard type oil, white Flora, for instance.

If you are making gravies, then butter definitely has the better taste.

Cookies are so much better when made with butter, but we should not be eating too many of them. If we are going to be naughty we might as well do it properly!

It is OK if these saturated fats are not part of our regular diet. Just an occasional treat.

Question 39

"What meat is best for a high protein diet?"

Sam McMaws

It really depends why you want to eat this kind of diet. If it is to lose weight, a high protein diet needs to be eaten in conjunction with a balance of other nutritionally rich foods, such as fruit and vegetables. Otherwise, your long term dietary needs will not be met.

As an athlete, again, it depends what kind of sport you are involved in. High protein will build muscle, but if you are involved in high intensity or endurance training, you need to keep up your levels of glycogen, which is the energy stored in your muscles. This means you need a fairly high level of carbohydrates in your diet.

Sports nutritionists recommend the following guidelines:

12 - 15% of daily calories from protein

25 - 30% of daily calories from fat

55 - 65% of daily calories from carbohydrate

Carbohydrates are needed for intense muscular effort. Fruit and energy drinks are a good source of simple carbs and provide quick energy. Things like whole grains, breads, cereal and pasta will help to boost the glycogen levels.

Protein rich foods are fish, chicken, turkey, meat, milk, tofu, yogurt, peanut butter, eggs and cheese.

Question 40

"What's a good nutritional, healthy snack during the day?"
Isobel Watt

One of the easiest things to carry around with you, would be some good quality dried fruit and some nuts. Almonds are highly recommended as they contain healthy fats and have been shown to be good for our hearts.

There are some good cereal bars on the market. Read the labels, to make sure they do not contain too much sugar or undesirable additives.

Bananas and apples will also give you a healthy burst of energy.

If you are feeling really healthy, carry some peeled carrots or celery sticks around with you in a container and have a munch on them.

Vegetables

Question 41

"What's the best way to mash potatoes?"

Owen Kay

for 2 people

- 2 - 3 large **potatoes**
- 1" cube of **butter**
- **salt** and **pepper**

1. Put some water on to boil.
2. Peel the potatoes and cut into 1" cubes.
3. Add to the boiling water, bring back to the boil, then turn down to simmer, for 10 minutes. The potatoes should be tender.
4. Drain and return to the pan.
5. Add the butter and the salt and pepper.
6. Mash with a potato masher or a fork.

Question 42

"What is the quickest and easiest way to cook a potato and how do u do it?? how long to cook it for, depending on size etc?"

Victoria Newlands

"How long should you cook a jacket potato for?"

Emily Atkinson

"What is the easiest vegetable to cook?"

James Black

"Baked potatoes, Microwave? oven? both? Why does it make those popping noises when you put it in the microwave?"

Dan Richter

The easiest vegetable to cook is a potato and the easiest way to cook it is to bake it in the oven.

Heat the oven to 200ºC fan oven/220ºC/Gas 7. If the potato is large, cook for 1 hour, medium 50 minutes, small 45 minutes. Don't forget to cut the skin across the top before putting it into the oven. Cooking at this temperature, and for this time, should give a tasty, crisp skin.

If you are in a hurry, place in the microwave on full power for 7 - 10 minutes. Don't forget to cut the skin.

Baked potatoes explode in the oven or the microwave, unless you make a cut in the skin. The skin goes dry and will eventually split or explode, hence the popping noises and the mess in the microwave or oven.

1 pre heat oven.

200°C | fan oven
220°C
gas 7

2 score potato

3 put in oven

50 mins
45

4 cut open

5 add

S P TUNA MAYO SWEETCORN OR

One classic filling for baked potatoes is tuna, sweetcorn and mayo, with some salt and pepper. Just mix everything together in proportions to your taste. You can use any excess in a sandwich the next day.

Another filling is to simply add a little olive oil spread to the potato and then add some grated cheese. This is really inexpensive and reasonably healthy, but just don't eat it all the time.

Question 43

"Red onions or white?" *Apurva Chitnis*

Red onions are slightly sweeter and milder than brown or white onions. You can use either when cooking. Red onions are useful to use in salads, whereas raw white onions would be a bit too strong.

"How do you chop onions without irritating your eyes?" *Nakul Pande*

"How do you stop onions making you cry?" *Simon Hammersley*

The reason onions make you cry is that they contain some sulphur. When you start to chop them, they then produce a gas called propanethial S-oxide. This gas reacts chemically with the water in your eyes, to form a weak sulphuric acid, so irritating your eyes and causing you to cry.

One way to stop crying is to put another source of water nearby, on your wrists, for example. The gas should react with that water and not with the water in your eyes. You could have a pan of boiling water nearby.

I have heard of people wearing swimming goggles to chop onions. This seems a little extreme.

Most of the problem comes from the root of the onions. See accross the page for instructions on cutting onions.

1. Cut the onion in half vertically. This means you cut through the root, but it is not exposed too much.

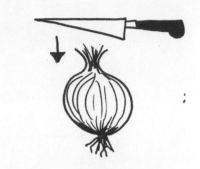

2. Peel back the brown outer skin of the onion, but don't tear it off. The root is still enclosed. Place the flat side of the onion down on the chopping board.

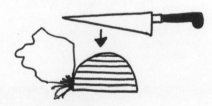

3. Cut into the onion, first with the point of the knife towards the root.

4. Now cut across the onion, leaving you with very small pieces.

5. Last of all cut off the root and discard.

Question 44

"What is the point of asparagus?"

George Pickering

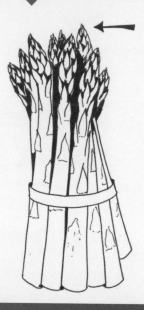

"How do you cook asparagus?"

Beatrice Fagan

1. First you need to break off the 'woody' ends of the asparagus stalk and discard them.
2. Lay in a frying pan and add enough boiling water just to cover it.
3. Simmer gently for 3 - 6 minutes, depending on how thick the asparagus is.
4. Drain and add a little butter.

Great with poached eggs, or just as a veg.

Question 45

"What is the best way to cook carrots, without them being too soft/hard?"

Lucy McColm

Here are some guidelines for cooking all vegetables. I am thinking that you may be interested in more than just carrots.

Depending on your taste, you do not always need to peel veggies. Washing them is a good idea. Larger things like potatoes and carrots need to be cut into pieces before cooking, broccoli broken into small 'trees' and so on.

Generally most vegetables need to be cooked in just enough water to cover them. Bring the water to the boil. Once boiling, add the vegetables and a little salt, bring back to the boil and simmer gently with the lid on the pan. If you keep the source of the heat low, not only will you preserve a little more nutrition in the vegetables, but you will also avoid burnt pans and very mucky cookers, where the pans have boiled over.

Here are some approximate cooking times:

- swedes and turnips — 20 - 25 minutes
- potatoes, parsnips, carrots — 10 - 15 minutes
- cauliflower — 10 minutes
- broccoli — 5 minutes, boiling gently
- green beans — 5 minutes
- sugar snaps — 2 minutes
- mangetout — 1 minute
- leeks — 5 minutes
- spinach — 30 seconds to 1 minute

For the spinach, you need just enough time to make the leaves wilt. You will only need a little water in the bottom of the pan.

- cabbage — 5 minutes

Again, you only need a little water, drain after cooking and add some butter and black pepper. Return to the pan and cook for another 2 minutes, to dry the cabbage a littlo.

"What is the best way to cut up vegetables?"

J Grantham

It really depends on what they are and what you are using them for.

One essential for chopping anything is a sharp knife. If your knife is blunt, you will find chopping very laborious.

Potatoes - if you are boiling or roasting them, cut into 2" chunks. If you are making potato wedges, cut them in half lengthways and then into long wedges.

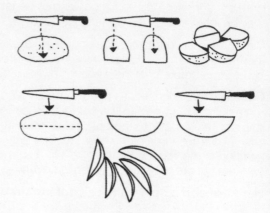

Carrots - if you are boiling them, cut them into round slices or long sticks. For salads, you can grate them. If you are using them for dips, cut into thin sticks.

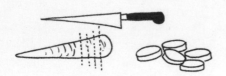

Tomatoes - cut into slices for sandwiches, wedges for salads.

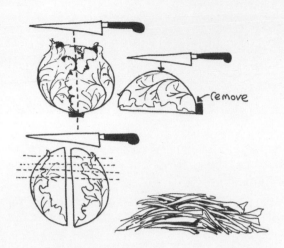

Cabbage - cut the whole cabbage in half vertically through the centre. Lay it flat on the board, cut in half again, lengthways, and then chop across each one, to produce thin strands of cabbage.

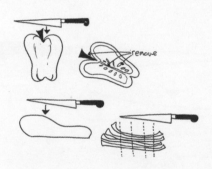

Peppers - first cut in half, lengthways and take out the seeds and the white bits. Slice them into thin slices, lengthways and depending what you are cooking, you can then cut them into small dice.

Brocolli and cauliflower - tear into small trees.

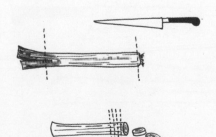

Leeks - cut off the root bit and then a good part of the darker green from the top. Slice into rings. Leeks are usually used as part of a recipe and not just on their own.

"After chopping chillies is there anything you can do to get it off your hands?"

Beth Pattison

It is very important to be careful when chopping chillies, that you do not touch your face, especially your eyes. You can wear disposable gloves if your hands are very sensitive.

Wash your hands immediately after chopping the chilli. Squeeze a little washing-up liquid into your hands and add about 1 teaspoon salt. Rub your hands together and then rinse. This is also a good way of getting other foody smells, fish for example, from your hands.

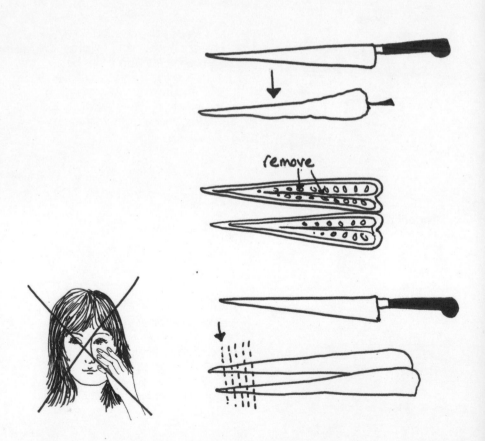

remove

Rice
&
Pasta

Question 46

"How do you stop pasta from sticking to the pan?" *Billie*

"How long should you cook pasta for and in how much water?" *Robert Masson*

Over-cooking pasta is the main cause of it sticking together in the pan. Boil enough water to completely cover the pasta and give it room to move in the pan. Add the pasta, bring back to the boil and then turn down to simmer gently for the appropriate time. Pasta is better a little 'al dente' (crisp to the bite), rather than soggy and overcooked.

Here is a guide, but it still depends on the thickness of the pasta:

Tagliatelle - the stuff that comes in little nests. 4 - 5 minutes.

Spaghetti - 6 minutes, depending how thick the spaghetti is.

Radiatore - looks like little radiators. 10 minutes.

Fusilli - little twists. 6 - 8 minutes.

Penne - little tubes, vary in size. 10 - 12 minutes.

Conchiglie - little shells. 6 - 8 minutes.

Macaroni - 12 - 15 minutes.

Farfalle - looks like little bows. 6 - 8 minutes.

Once you have drained the pasta, you can add a little olive oil or butter. Gently stir the pasta, to distribute the oil and place a lid over the pan. It will keep warm for 10 minutes or so.

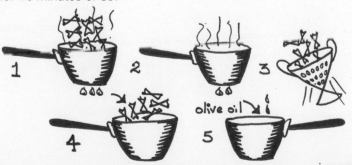

Question 47

"How do you make perfect rice? Mine is always so sticky and stodgy!"

James Crowe

"What is the best way to stop rice sticking together?"

Sam MacMaws

I would recommend using basmati rice - it is the easiest to cook and gives the best results. Here is a method which I find foolproof. It will serve 2 people with good appetites.

1. Put 2 mugs of water in a saucepan and bring to the boil.
2. Add 1 mug of basmati rice and stir once. Bring back to the boil and then turn down to simmer very gently. Put a lid on the pan and simmer for 12 - 15 minutes, until all the liquid has been absorbed. Don't stir the rice again during the cooking time.

The rice should be light and fluffy.

If you want to use pilau rice seasoning, add it along with the rice, once the water is boiling. Add 1 teaspoon for 2 people.

water

rice

12 - 15 minutes

Question 48

"What is the difference between rices and what's best for you?" *Ben Stanyon*

"Does brown rice take longer to cook than white rice? What are the differences?" *Josh Garwood*

To produce brown rice, only the outer layer (hull) of the rice grain is removed. The production of white rice involves milling and polishing and destroys lots of the vitamins and minerals. Also, all of the dietary fibre and essential fatty acids is lost. Some white rice has some vitamins and minerals added after processing. The oil in brown rice helps to lower cholesterol.

We can, therefore, come to the conclusion that brown rice is much healthier for us to eat. It also has a nutty taste, whereas white rice can be quite bland. It is, however, a little bit more difficult to cook and it takes longer.

Here is a method for cooking brown rice:

1. Boil 2 mugs of water in a saucepan.
2. Add 1 mug rice, bring back to the boil and then turn down to simmer gently. Place a lid on the pan.
3. Simmer gently for 40 - 45 minutes, until the rice is tender and has absorbed all the water. If the water boils away before the rice is tender, just add a little more water.

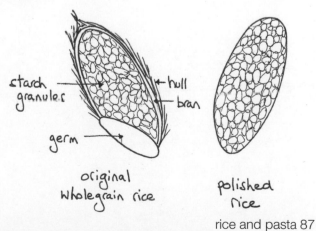

starch granules — hull — bran — germ

original wholegrain rice

polished rice

Eggs

Question 49

"How do you crack an egg without breaking the yolk?"
Andrew Muress

"What's the best way to crack an egg?"
Jasmine Cunningham

Gently, would be the first answer!

2 ways:

1. If you have 2 eggs, gently tap them together, only one of them will break and should leave a circular crack. Place both thumbs in the crack, don't push your thumbs through the egg, but pull the shell apart. The yolk should come out whole.

2. If you just have the one egg, gently tap the egg on a work surface corner, or on the edge of a pan or bowl, keep turning the egg and make a crack in the egg about 1" long. Place both thumbs into the crack and gently pull apart.

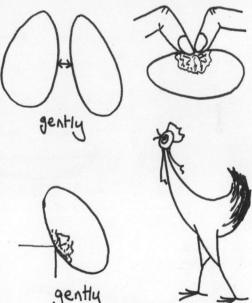

Question 50

> "What are all the things you can do with an egg?"
>
> *Dan Richter*

There are quite a few suggestions within the next questions. In addition, you can also fry them. Although this is not the healthiest way to cook them, fried egg butties make great supper snacks. Here's how to fry an egg:

1. Break the egg into a mug.
2. Heat 1" cube of butter in the frying pan, until the butter just bubbles.
3. Gently pour the egg into the frying pan.
4. Cook on medium heat, until the egg is set. Season well with salt and pepper.

If you want 'easy over' hard yolk, using a slotted turner, turn the egg over half-way through cooking.

Question 51

"How do you cook perfect eggie bread?"

Joe Midgley

To make 1 slice of eggie bread, you will need one egg, one thick slice of bread, a little butter or spread and some salt and pepper.

1. Beat the egg with a fork and season with salt and pepper. Pour onto a plate.
2. Dip both sides of the the bread into the egg, making sure all the bread is covered with the egg mixture.
3. Heat a little butter or spread in a frying pan. Add the eggie bread and cook on a medium heat, until browned. Turn over and brown the other side.

Serve with baked beans, tomatoes or just HP sauce.

Question 52

"What can you have with omelettes?"

Joseph Dakkah

"What is the quickest way to make an omelette and what are good things to add?"

Sam MacMaws

"How do you make a good omelette?"

William Bennett

Instructions for a basic omelette for 1 person:

1. Break three eggs into a mug and beat well with a fork. Add two tablespoons of water.
2. Switch on the grill to full heat, to warm up.
3. Melt 2 x 1" cubes of butter in the frying pan. Once it begins to 'bubble', pour the egg mixture into the pan.
4. As it sets on the bottom of the pan, gently move the set egg with a fish slice and allow the runny egg to take its place. Do this with two or three sweeping movements; don't stir, or you will get scrambled egg.
5. While there is still a little runny egg on the top, take off the heat and add whatever filling you want. Top with cheese (not essential) and place the frying pan under the hot grill. Watch carefully, the omelette should rise.
6. Once it is browned on the top, remove from the grill and turn out onto a plate. Serve with salad, garlic bread or baked potatoes.

Suggested fillings - cheese, tomato, mushrooms, fried onions, crispy grilled bacon cut into pieces, cooked chicken, ham or any combination of these ingredients.

Question 53

"Is it true that when poaching an egg you should do it in constantly stirred or swirling water?" *Jelle Zemstra*

"How do you make poached egg without it going all messy?" *Isra Rehman*

No, you do not need to stir the water.

1. Using a small pan or frying pan, half fill with water and add a good pinch of salt. Bring to the boil, then turn down until the water is just simmering gently.
2. Break the egg into a mug or cup and gently pour into the water. Do not stir or turn the heat up, just let it cook gently. It will take 2 - 4 minutes, depending on the size of the egg.

3. Once the egg has gone opaque, gently lift out with a slotted turner and let the water drain from it.
4. Great with beans on toast, tomato sauce or HP.

The secret to good poached eggs is to use very fresh eggs.

Question 54

"How long does it actually take to boil an egg?"
Laura Elliot & Theo Brumhead

1. Using a small pan, fill ⅔ full with water and bring to the boil.
2. Lower the egg into the pan on a spoon.
3. Time from the point you put the egg into the boiling water. Simmer briskly for 3 minutes for a very runny egg; 5 minutes and you will still be able to dip your soldiers in the runny yolk; 12 minutes and it will be hard-boiled.

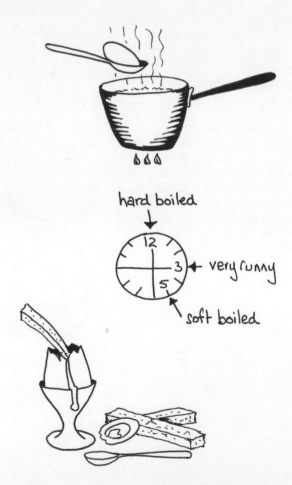

Question 55

"Is it best to cook scrambled egg in the microwave or a pan?"

Greg Lound

I think it is always best to cook things on the hob. If you cook scrambled egg in the microwave, you will still need to stand by it, open the door and stir the egg. It becomes hard in parts and runny in others. Eggs can easily become rubbery. You have much more control when you can see the egg mixture in the pan and it is quicker. Here is a simple method:

1. Using a small milk pan, preferably non-stick, add 1" cube of butter, heat gently until the butter bubbles.
2. Break the egg into the pan and add salt and pepper. Stir slowly, breaking up the egg yolk.
3. Stir until the egg is almost set, take off the heat and turn out into a bowl or plate. The egg will continue to cook in its own heat. If you cook it too long, it will become rubbery.
4. You can add grated cheese and/ or a chopped-up tomato halfway through the cooking.

Question 56

"Realistically, how long can I keep eggs past their use-by date? I usually go for 2 weeks but never know if this is ok!"

Daniella Gore

General consensus is - don't eat eggs after their best-before date/use-by date. There is a tendency to think that eggs are enclosed in their shells and therefore impervious to deterioration. Not true.

Their use-by date is usually one month from laying. Eggs are not the most expensive thing to buy, so don't take the risk. Check when you are buying eggs that they have not been on the shelf in the store for too long.

Keep eggs in the fridge in their box. If, when you get them home, one is cracked and you had not noticed in the shop, throw it away.

How To
Cook
Things

Question 57

> ## "What is the best way to season normally bland ingredients like noodles?"
>
> *Jack Falkingham*

Noodles are usually part of some kind of stir fry. You can vary the different sauces which you add. Things like hoisin, teriyaki and soy are the classics.

Here is a basic noodle recipe, you can add or take away vegetables.

Hoisin Noodles   Serves 2

- 1 **chicken breast**, cut into thin strips
- 1 teaspoon grated **fresh ginger**
- 1 clove **garlic**, finely chopped
- ½ x 400g pack of **fresh egg noodles** or **straight-to-wok noodles**
- ½ x 340g can **sweetcorn**

- 3 **mushrooms**, sliced
- 3 spring **onions**, sliced
- 1½ mugs boiling **water** + 1 teaspoon **concentrated chicken stock**
- 1 teaspoon **soy sauce**
- 2 tablespoons **hoisin sauce**
- 1 tablespoon **oil**

1. Heat the oil in a wok. Add the onions, ginger and garlic. Fry for 30 seconds.
2. Add the chicken to the wok and stir fry for 1 minute.
3. Add the mushrooms and stir fry for 30 seconds.
4. Add the water, stock, soy, hoisin, sweetcorn and noodles. Bring to the boil, then turn down to simmer for 1 minute.
5. Season well and serve in individual bowls.

Question 58

To make egg and chicken fried rice for 2 people you will need:-

- 1½ mugs **basmati rice**
- 1 teaspoon **pilau rice seasoning**
- 1 **chicken breast**
- 2 **eggs**, beaten
- 1 **onion**, finely chopped
- 1 **red pepper**, chopped finely
- 1 small clove **garlic**, finely chopped
- **oil** to fry

1. To cook the rice, put 3 mugs of water on to boil. Once boiling, add the pilau rice seasoning and the rice. Stir just once. Simmer for 10 - 15 minutes, until all the water has been absorbed by the rice. Leave to one side until needed.
2. Pan roast the chicken breast. Heat a little oil in a frying pan and add the chicken breast. Cook on a high heat for 2 minutes each side. Turn the heat down to medium and cook, with a lid on, for a further 4 minutes each side. If you have a very small chicken breast, you will only need 3 minutes each side. Leave to one side until needed.
3. Heat a little oil in a wok. Add the beaten eggs. Swish around the pan so it forms a very thin omelette. Cook for about 30 seconds, or until the egg is no longer runny, but not rubbery. Take out of the wok and leave to one side until needed.
4. Add a little more oil to the pan and heat. Add the onions, garlic and peppers and fry until they begin to brown.
5. Add the rice to the pan and stir fry for 1 minute. Take off the heat.
6. Cut the chicken into small pieces. Add to the pan.
7. Cut the egg into strips. Add to the pan and season well with salt and pepper.

Question 59

> ## "What is a really quick and easy way to make GOOD pancakes?"
> *Kirsty Crooks*

This is a great and foolproof recipe and can be scaled up if you have friends around. Pancakes are good fun to make for a crowd. You can serve them simply with lemon juice and sugar, bananas and cream, ice cream, chocolate sauce (see page 112), or fruit etc.

Makes about 6

- 2 **eggs**
- 6 tablespoons **plain flour**
- **milk**
- **Trex** or **white Flora** to fry (you can use oil, but a lard type is best)

1. Beat the eggs and flour together in a bowl or jug. Gradually add the milk, making sure there are no lumps. The mixture should be as thin as single cream, i.e. quite thin, but not as thin as milk.
2. Heat about ½" cube of lard in a frying pan. When the fat begins to have a little heat haze, pour approximately 2 tablespoons of the mixture into the pan. Tip the pan around, so that the mixture spreads over the surface of the pan. Let the mixture cook for about 1 minute.
3. Gently lift the edge of the pancake to see if it is browned. Once browned, turn the pancake with a slotted turner, or toss and then cook the other side.

Question 60

"How would I know when a steak is cooked medium rare?"
Rob Dalziel

"How do I cook the perfect steak? I like rare... Talk to me!"
Nathan Clements

"What are the different times for cooking a steak, rare, medium rare etc.?"
Beatrice Fagan

I am surprised so many have asked how to cook a steak, I thought students were supposed to be broke! The recipe opposite will cost about £5.70 per person.

	high heat	medium heat
RARE	2 each side	2 each side
MEDIUM RARE	2 each side	4 each side
WELL DONE	2 each side	6 each side

Beef Steak with Mash and Mustard Sauce

Time 35 minutes, Serves 2

Mustard sauce

- 2 tablespoons **crème fraîche** or **soured cream**
- 1 tablespoon **wholegrain mustard**
- **salt** and **pepper**

Mash

- 4 medium **potatoes**, peeled
- 1" cube of **butter**
- **salt** and **pepper**

- 2 **beef steaks**, either fillet, topside or rump, about 1" thick.
- **oil** to fry

1. To make the mustard sauce, simply mix the crème fraîche and mustard together. Leave in the fridge until needed.
2. Put the water on to boil for the mash. Cut the potatoes into 2" chunks. Put in the boiling water and bring to the boil. Then turn down to simmer for 10 - 15 minutes until tender.
3. Once the potatoes are cooked, drain and return to the pan. Add the butter and mash. Leave with the lid on until needed.
4. Heat a little oil in a frying pan. Have the heat quite high and when the oil begins to have a heat haze above it (it does not need to smoke), add the steaks.
5. For a rare steak, cook on this high heat for 2 minutes each side, then turn down to a medium heat for a further 2 minutes each side.
6. For a medium steak, cook on this high heat for 2 minutes each side, then turn down to a medium heat for a further 4 minutes each side.
7. For a well-done steak, cook on this high heat for 2 minutes each side, then turn down to a medium heat for a further 6 minutes each side. Serve the steak with the mash and the mustard sauce.

The above timings are for a 1" thick steak, but, if the steak is thinner, cook for less time.

Question 61

"Can you give me reliable roast dinner timings please? Something is always raw or burned...."

Jenny Copperwheat

This would really impress mum and dad when they come to visit you. Get someone to help you, especially the first time you attempt it.

Cooking time 3½ hours, Serves 4

Brisket is one of the cheapest joints of beef that you can buy. It needs to be cooked for a longer time, but can be delicious.

- 2 kg piece of **beef brisket**
- sprig **rosemary** or 1 teaspoon **dried rosemary**
- 1 mug **water** + 1 tablespoon **liquid beef stock** or 1 **stock cube**
- a little **oil**
- 6 - 8 medium **potatoes**
- 1 **onion**, cut into wedges
- 6 - 8 **carrots**
- 1" cube **butter**.
- **green vegetables**

Gravy

- 1 tablespoon **flour**
- 1 tablespoon softened **butter**

1. Preheat the oven to 180°C fan oven/ 200°C/Gas 6.
2. Put the meat in a casserole dish. Place the sprigs of rosemary under the strings holding the meat together. Add the water and stock and brush the top of the meat with oil. Season well and cover with a lid or foil. Place in the preheated oven for 1 hour.
3. After 1 hour, turn the oven down to 150°C and cook for a further 2 ½ hours. During that time, the vegetables need to be cooked. See steps 4 - 6.
4. Cut the potatoes into quarters and place on a baking tray, together with the onion wedges. Drizzle with oil, season with salt and pepper and mix together with your hands. One hour before the end of the cooking time for the meat, turn up the oven to 180°C fan oven/ 200°C/Gas 6 and put the potatoes in the oven.

5. Peel the carrots and cut into sticks. Place in an ovenproof dish with the butter and ¼ mug water. Cover with foil and place in the oven 30 minutes before the end of the cooking time for the meat.
6. Put water on to boil for the green vegetables. When the cooking time for the meat is finished, put the green vegetables on to boil. Simmer broccoli for 4 - 5 minutes, green beans for 8 - 10 minutes.
7. Take the meat out of the oven. If the potatoes and carrots are cooked, turn the oven down to keep them warm.
8. Take the meat out of the casserole dish and place on a board, ready to carve. Leave to stand while you cook the gravy.
9. To make the gravy, pour the rest of the contents of the casserole dish into a saucepan. In a bowl, mix the butter and flour to a paste, add to the meat juices and stir well. Bring the gravy to the boil, and simmer for 1 - 2 minutes. If the gravy is too thick, add a little water from the vegetables you have cooked.
10. Carve the meat and serve with the vegetables and the gravy.

Time line to serve the meal at 1.30 p.m.

- **9.30 a.m.** Put oven on to heat @ 180°C fan oven/200°C/Gas 6.
- **9.45 a.m.** Put meat in the oven.
- **10.45 a.m**. Turn oven down to 150°C fan oven/ 170°C/Gas 4.
- **12.15 a.m.** Turn the oven back up to 180°C fan oven/ 200°C/Gas 6 and put the potatoes in.
- **12.45 p.m.** Put carrots in the oven.
- **1.15 p.m.** Put greens on to cook.
- **1.15 p.m.** Take meat out of the oven.
- **1.20 p.m.** Drain the greens, and leave in pan to stay warm.
- **1.22 p.m.** Make the gravy, then carve the meat.
- **1.30 p.m.** ish Serve

Use boiled water from a kettle for your vegetables, as this will speed things up.

If you need to add any liquid to the gravy, make sure you use water from the boiled vegetables. There is lots of flavour there.

Question 62

"How can you get Sunday lunch experience in student halls on a student budget?"

Jack Falkingham

This is not quite a Sunday lunch, but you do get the roast potatoes and it is inexpensive. You can possibly try the recipe on the roast dinner page 104, when you are house sharing, but get a bit of cooking experience first. The recipe below can be done in student halls. You only need a big casserole dish, or roasting tray.

Roast Potatoes and Sausages

Serves 2   Preparation time 5 minutes, cooking time 1 hour

- 4 - 6 **potatoes**
- 1 **onion**
- 1 tablespoon cooking **oil**
- 6 - 8 **sausages**, beef, pork or vegetarian
- **salt** and **pepper**

1. Preheat the oven to 180°C fan oven/200°C/Gas 6.
2. Wash potatoes and cut into large wedges. Peel the onion and cut into 6.
3. Oil the casserole dish or baking tray and place the potatoes, sausages and onions in it. Brush everything with the oil (use your fingers if you do not have a brush) and season well with salt and pepper.
4. Put in the oven for 30 minutes. Take out of the oven and carefully turn things over, so that they brown on the other side. Cook for a further 20 - 30 minutes, or until everything is browned.
5. Serve with baked beans.

180℃ fan / 200℃ / gas 6 = 30 mins

Turn everything + another 20-30 mins

Question 63

> "How do you make soup from scratch?"
>
> *Claire Sampson*

Soup is very easy to make and a great way of learning how to cook. Here is a recipe for a very simple, inexpensive vegetable soup

Vegetable Soup

- 1" cube **butter**
- ½ medium **onion**, chopped
- 1 small **potato**, cut into cubes
- 1 stick of **celery**, cut into pieces
- 1 medium sized **carrot**, peeled and sliced
- 1 dessertspoon **flour**
- 1½ mugs **water**
- ½ **vegetable** or **chicken stock cube**
- ¼ mug frozen **peas**
- 1 slice of **ham**, chopped (optional)
- **salt** and **pepper**

1. Heat the butter in a saucepan and fry the onion for 1 minute.
2. Add the potatoes, celery and carrots and cook for about 1 minute.
3. Add flour and mix in with the vegetables already in the pan.
4. Add the water and stock cube and bring to the boil. Simmer for 10 minutes, or until the vegetables are cooked.
5. Add the peas and cook for 2 minutes.
6. Add the pieces of ham and cook for 1 minute.
7. Serve with bread.

French Onion Soup

French onion soup is inexpensive to make, and the caramelized onions taste delicious. You need to watch the onions as they brown and stir them frequently; but the end result is worth the effort. The cheesy croutons make a good contrast of flavour.

Serves 2

- ○ 1 large **onion**, sliced
- ○ 1½ tablespoons **oil** to fry
- ○ 1½ mugs **water** + 1 vegetable **stock cube**
- ○ ½ teaspoon **marmite**
- ○ **salt** and **pepper**

Cheesy croutons

- ○ 1 slice **wholemeal bread**
- ○ ¼ mug **grated cheese**

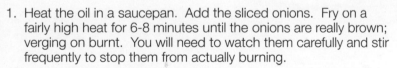

1. Heat the oil in a saucepan. Add the sliced onions. Fry on a fairly high heat for 6-8 minutes until the onions are really brown; verging on burnt. You will need to watch them carefully and stir frequently to stop them from actually burning.

2. Once the onions are really brown add the water, crumbled stock cube, and marmite. Bring to the boil, and then turn down to simmer for 10 minutes.

3. While the soup is cooking, make some cheese on toast. You will not need to butter the toast. Once toasted, cut into squares to use as croutons.

4. Taste the soup and season. Pour into a bowl and drop the croutons on top.

Question 64

"How do I cook my chicken without it becoming dry?"

Katy Dickinson

"What is the best way to fry chicken, without over or under cooking it?"

Emily Summer

One good way to cook chicken breast is to **pan roast** it.

1. Heat a little oil in a frying pan, add the chicken breast and cook on a high heat for 2 minutes each side.
2. Turn down to a medium heat, put a lid or some foil over the chicken and cook for 4 minutes each side. Check to see if it cooked through by making an insert into the thickest part of the chicken. It should not be pink and clear juices should run from it.

2 minutes each side

4 minutes each side

It is very useful and economical to **roast** a whole chicken. You can eat it freshly cooked for one meal and have the leftovers in sandwiches etc. If you are just cooking for yourself, get a 2 Kg chicken.

1. Preheat the oven to 180°C fan oven/200°C/Gas 6.
2. Wash the chicken and make sure it does not have anything in the cavity.
3. Grease a casserole dish, or roasting tin. Place the chicken in the dish and pour some oil over the top. Distribute it over the surface of the chicken, using your hands.
4. Season well with salt and pepper.
5. Cover with a lid or some foil and place in the oven, for 1 hour.
6. After one hour, take off the lid or foil and cook for a further 35 - 45 minutes, until the chicken is browned.
7. If you have a 3 Kg chicken, cook for 1½ hours before removing the foil; for a 4 Kg chicken 2 hours. Any size chicken should brown in 35 - 45 minutes.
8. You can check to see that the chicken is done by inserting a knife into the chicken breast, near the leg. Squash the chicken and the juices should be clear and not have any redness in them.

2 kg chicken

Olive oil + salt pepper

+ Water

+foil

180°c fan oven
200°C
gas 6
= 1 hour

Remove foil
+
35-40 mins

Question 65

This is a very quick and easy way to make chocolate sauce and has a much better taste than bought stuff. It is great to use with ice cream as a dessert for lots of people, or as a video snack.

Chocolate sauce

- ¼ x 500g pack **butter**
- 4 heaped tablespoons **sugar** (brown or white)
- 3 heaped tablespoons **drinking chocolate**
- 2 tablespoons **milk** or **cream**

1. Place the butter, sugar and chocolate in a saucepan. Heat gently, stir well and allow to simmer for 1 minute.
2. Add the milk or cream carefully, as it may spit at you! Simmer for another 1 minute, stirring all the time. It should be smooth and thick by now.
3. Allow to cool slightly, before serving on top of the ice cream. You will need to leave the sauce to cool longer, if you are using glass dishes, as the contrast in temperature between the sauce and the ice cream may break thinner glass.

Question 66

"I keep trying to make Victoria sponge, but it's always thin and dry. I'm becoming a bit of a cake-baking joke. Do you have a reliable recipe that even I can make?"

Jenny Copperwheat

There may be a couple of reasons why the cakes you are cooking are dry and flat. Are you using self-raising flour? Is your oven preheated to the correct temperature? If you have an old oven, it is worth getting an oven thermometer and checking exactly what temperature you are cooking at.

Many of you will not have weighing scales, so I have used mug measures. The mug should be approximately ½ pint.

You can buy a food mixer from the supermarket, for about £12. If you are intending to make lots of cakes, this is a worthwhile investment.

Victoria Sponge

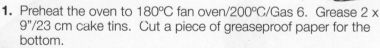

- 225g softened **butter** (left out of the fridge for a couple of hours)
- ¾ mug **sugar**
- 4 **eggs**
- 1 teaspoon **vanilla extract**
- 1½ mugs **self-raising flour**
- 3 tablespoons **water**

1. Preheat the oven to 180°C fan oven/200°C/Gas 6. Grease 2 x 9"/23 cm cake tins. Cut a piece of greaseproof paper for the bottom.
2. Beat together the butter and sugar until it is quite light and fluffy.
3. Add the eggs, one at a time, and beat into the mixture.
4. Add the vanilla extract and mix.
5. Add the flour and the water. Fold in gently and do not beat. Mix until smooth.
6. Divide between the two cake tins. Flatten out the mixture.
7. Place in the oven for 20 - 25 minutes. When cooked, the cake should 'bounce back' when pressed gently.
8. Once the cakes are cooled, sandwich together with whipped cream and jam.

Question 67

You can make ice cream without a machine, but it is a little tedious and time consuming. However, it will taste delicious. So, if you have the time, here is one way:

Vanilla ice cream

- ○ 1 mug **milk**
- ○ 1 mug **double cream**
- ○ 1 teaspoon **vanilla extract**
- ○ 4 **egg yolks**
- ○ ½ mug **sugar**

1. Put the milk and cream in a saucepan, bring to the boil and take off the heat. Add the vanilla extract.
2. Put the egg yolks and the sugar in a large bowl and beat well until the mixture begins to thicken.
3. Pour the hot milk and cream into the bowl and stir well.
4. Return to the saucepan and heat very gently, do not allow the mixture to boil or you will have scrambled eggs!
5. Once it has thickened slightly, take off the heat and leave to cool.
6. Place in a container that will eventually go in the freezer and chill in the fridge for 2 hours.
7. Transfer to the freezer for 1 hour.
8. Take out and beat the ice cream, to break up any crystals that are beginning to form.
9. Return to the freezer for another hour and then beat again.
10. Repeat step 9 three times and you should have some tasty ice cream, plus a lot of patience!

Question 68

"What is the best way to cook couscous?"

Emily Summer

Couscous is very easy to cook and versatile. However, it can be a bit bland, if just cooked on its own. One easy thing to do is to add a veggie stock cube to the water you soak the couscous in. You can add other things like ground cumin, chopped up spring onion, or finely chopped courgettes.

You will need a bowl and a plate big enough to cover the bowl. To feed 2, place 1 mug of couscous in the bowl mixed with anything else you want to add to it. Boil the kettle and add 2 mugs of boiling water to the couscous. Cover with a plate and leave for 5 minutes, until all the water has been absorbed.

leave to stand for 5 minutes

Question 69

> "If you don't like to fry things, what's the best way to cook things like sausage and bacon?"
>
> *Charlotte Parkinson*

> "What is the healthiest way to cook bacon?"
>
> *Henry Waine*

> "What is the quickest way to cook bacon?"
>
> *James Black*

> Is it healthier to grill or fry bacon and what are the differences?
>
> *Kyle Daniel*

The quickest way to cook sausages and bacon is to fry them. Bacon and sausages already contain quite a bit of fat, so it's best not to add more to them in the cooking process. So, if you do fry them, add just a very small amount of sunflower oil. It is also good to drain them on some kitchen paper before serving them.

There are two ways to avoid frying bacon and sausages:

- Grill them. Bear in mind that the sausages will take longer to cook than the bacon, so start the sausages about 10 minutes before the bacon and turn frequently.
- An easier way is to cook them in the oven:
1. Preheat the oven to 200ºC fan oven/220ºC/Gas 7.
2. Lightly grease a non-stick baking tray. Put the sausages on one tray and put in the oven.
3. After 15 minutes, put the bacon on a tray and put in the oven. Cook for a further 10 minutes.

Question 70

Chicken Curry

Serves 2   Preparation and cooking time 20 minutes

- 1 **onion**, chopped
- 1 **potato**, cut into ½" cubes
- 1 dessertspoon **cooking oil**
- 2 **chicken** breasts
- 2 teaspoons **flour**
- 3 cloves **garlic**, finely chopped
- 1 mug **water**
- 4 teaspoons mild **curry paste** (use less if the curry paste is hot)
- 1 **chicken stock cube**, crumbled
- ½ mug **natural yogurt**

1. Fry the onion and potato in the oil.
2. Cut the chicken breasts into pieces and add to the pan. Cook for 2 - 3 minutes, until the chicken is no longer pink on the outside.
3. Add the flour and stir well. Add the garlic, water, curry paste and stock cube. Stir well.
4. Bring to the boil and then simmer for 10 - 15 minutes, until the chicken and the vegetables are cooked.
5. Stir in the yogurt, but do not let it boil. Cook gently for 1 minute.
6. Serve with rice (see page 86).

Question 71

"How do you create really crispy, roast potatoes, but not burn them?"

Charlotte Maguiness

"How long do you roast vegetables for before they are done?" *Charlotte Parkinson*

"How do I cook perfect roast potatoes?"

Katy Dickinson

Roast Potatoes, the easy way

1. Preheat the oven to 180°C fan oven/200°C/Gas 6. Cut the potatoes into 2 - 3" chunks. You do not need to peel the potatoes.
2. Place them on a baking tray. Sprinkle with salt and oil. If you have some fresh rosemary, pull off the leaves and sprinkle over the potatoes (dried rosemary will also work fine).
3. Using your hands, make sure the oil is evenly distributed around the potatoes. Make sure that the potatoes are not flat side down, this will mean more of the potatoes will brown.
4. Cook in the oven for 45 - 50 minutes, until they are brown.

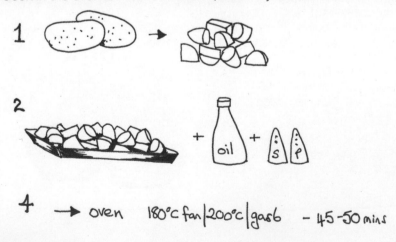

Posh roast potatoes

1. Preheat the oven to 180°C fan oven/200°C/Gas 6.
2. Peel the potatoes. Cut into 2 - 3" chunks.
3. Place in a pan of boiling water and cook for 10 minutes. Drain the water from the pan.
4. Add salt and oil to the pan, put the lid on the pan and shake it quite vigorously. This will cause the outsides of the potatoes to become a little furry and will also distribute the oil and salt.
5. Place on a well greased baking tray and cook for 45 - 50 minutes, until browned.

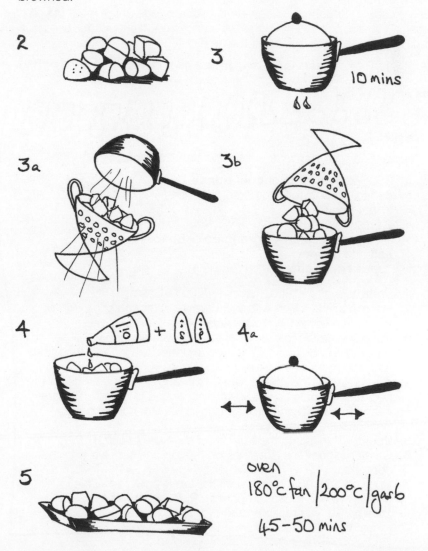

Question 72

There are many recipes which use mince and it is one of the most versatile meats to cook. Spaghetti Bolognese is probably one of the most popular amongst students. It is great because you can cook enough for two days and eat half when you cook it and half the next day.

Shepherd's Pie is another dish using mince and here is my simple method.

Serves 2

Preparation time 20 minutes, cooking time 25 minutes

- 250g pack of **lamb** or **beef mince**
- 6 medium **potatoes**, cut into ½" cubes
- ½ mug **water**
- 2 teaspoons **butter**
- 1 dessertspoon **gravy granules** or **Bisto**
- **salt** and **pepper**
- 1 mug grated **cheese**

1. Preheat oven to 180°C fan oven/200°C/Gas 6.
2. Put mince into a pan with the ½ mug water and bring to the boil. Simmer for 10 - 15 minutes.
3. Put diced potatoes in a separate pan with enough water to cover them. Boil for 10 minutes and then drain. Add the butter and mix.
4. Add gravy powder to the meat, following the instructions on the packet of granules as they differ according to brand. The gravy needs to be thickened to the consistency of double cream. Season with salt and pepper.
5. Pour the mince into the bottom of a casserole dish.
6. Carefully spoon the potatoes on the top and sprinkle with the cheese.
7. Cook for 20 - 25 minutes until the top is browned. This is an easy way to make Shepherd's Pie without using mashed potatoes. If you make enough for two, this dish is ideal to reheat the next day.

1

180°c fan oven
200°c
gas 6

2

mince + water +

MINCE

10-15 mins

3

diced potatoes = 10 mins

3a

3b

potatoes + butter & mix.

4

+gravy granules & stir

MINCE

6

5

mince

potatoes + grated cheese

7 → oven 20-25 mins

How Long
To Cook
Things

Question 73

"How can you tell when food is cooked?"
Emily Norman

If you are an inexperienced cook, it is best to follow directions from a good, simple cookbook. Invest in some kind of timer with an alarm on it; they can be very inexpensive. If you are cooking pre-prepared foods, follow the instructions on the pack.

If you are living in student accommodation, you may have a very old cooker. If you find that everything is overdone, or underdone, invest in an oven thermometer; they are less than £5. Set the oven to 180°C fan oven/200°C/ Gas 6. Put the thermometer in the oven and see what the temperature actually is. After this, you can adjust all your oven settings accordingly.

The following questions give more specific answers regarding the appearance of food when it is properly cooked.

Question 74

> "How do you know when something is cooked? For example, chicken?"
>
> *Joseph Dakkah*

> "How do you know when chicken is cooked properly?"
>
> *Rob Gainer*

> "What meats are OK to eat if they are a little bit pink and which ones need to be cooked through?"
>
> *Beth Pattison*

Chicken should not be eaten when it is at all pink in the middle. The best way to check, is to get a sharp knife and cut through the thickest part of the meat and check it is not pink inside.

If you **roast a chicken** and want to check that it is cooked through, make a cut with a sharp knife into the breast of the chicken and squash a little to make juices flow. If they run pink, then the chicken is not cooked. If the juices are clear, you are OK.

If you are cooking **beef steak**, follow the instructions on page 103. If you are cooking beef mince, the mince will change colour as it is cooked and will go from red to a brown colour. Even when cooking **mince (beef, pork or lamb)**, you need to allow a little time for the meat to become tender and for the flavours to develop in the dish. See "Nosh4student" for Spaghetti Bolognese, or page 120 for Shepherd's Pie.

If you are cooking **stewing beef or lamb**, it needs to be slow cooked and will take about 1½ hours to become tender. It is safe to eat once it it no longer red, but, if you want it good and tender, you will need to wait for a while.

Be very careful with pork. If you cook a **pork steak or chop,** you will need to cook on a high heat, for 2 minutes each side and then turn down to a lower heat, for 3 - 4 minutes each side, depending how thick the meat is. If you press the steak or chop and the juices are clear, it should be OK, but it is best to check by making a little cut into the meat and making sure is it not pink inside. It is a bit more difficult to tell when a pork steak is done, because it will still look a little pink.

Fish is much easier. **White fish** is opaque, when it is raw and becomes white when cooked. Be careful not to overcook fish, as it can soon become dry and rubbery. **Salmon and trout** are pink and opaque. They stay pink, but lose the opaque look and will easily 'flake' (pull apart), when cooked. The flakes will hold together when they are not cooked through.

> # "To what extent can you eat raw meat?"
> *Todd Rayner*

The only absolutely raw meat you could eat would be an Italian Beef Carpaccio. It is made from impeccable, thinly shaved meat and served with a vinaigrette dressing. This is not something to be attempted at home.

You can eat steak that is rare, but the steak has been heated and should not be 'raw'.

> # "What happens if you eat raw meat?"
> *Rob Gainer*

You may well get food poisoning. Raw meat can become contaminated at any stage in the process before you buy it and begin to cook it. Usually, any contamination is destroyed as the meat is cooked thoroughly.

RAW IS OK WITH ME

Question 75

"How to tell when a sausage is cooked properly?"

Emily Swallow

Sausages should not be cooked too quickly, otherwise they can be browned on the outside and not cooked on the inside. This happens especially when you are frying them. Keep the heat down to medium. Keep turning the sausages. If they are thin, they will usually be cooked by the time the outside is browned. If they are chunky, you will need to take care. The easiest way to see if they are done, is to cut one in half. The meat starts off pink and when cooked, will still look pale, but it should have turned a pale brown colour.

Question 76

> "When cooking a pizza, how do you know when it is ready?"
>
> *John Woodal*

Assuming that you are cooking a ready-made pizza, make sure the oven is preheated to the correct temperature. Cook for the suggested time. The pizza should be a little brown around the edges and the cheese bubbling slightly.

If you are making your own pizza, you will be following a recipe and the timings will be different if you have a thick or thin base. Again, the top should be browned slightly and the cheese bubbling. If you are adding any meats to the topping, they will be cut quite small and should be cooked in the time it takes the base to cook.

Question 77

> ## "How can you tell when breaded chicken or fish is cooked?"
> *Tom Dons*

When you are cooking pre-prepared foods, such as breaded chicken and fish, follow the instructions on the packet carefully.

Always preheat the oven, that is, bring the oven up to the correct temperature before putting the food in the oven. Usually there is a light near the oven controls, that goes off when the oven is up to the right temperature.

Use a timer. Don't guess what time you put the stuff in.

If you are still unsure, take a knife and fork and gently open the chicken or the fish. Fish should look white and no longer opaque. Chicken should be white and no longer pink.

> ## "How do you cook fish?"
> *Ben Stanyon*
>
> ## "How can you tell when fish is done?"
> *Charlotte Parkinson*

Before you cook fish, it is opaque and grey. When it is cooked, it becomes white. If you cook it too long, it easily becomes dry and rubbery.

It is best to follow a recipe when cooking fish. Just frying it on the hob is not the best and will make your house smell for quite a while. If you poach it on the hob with a little milk, make sure you put a lid on the pan (see page 67). The time it takes to cook depends on the thickness of the fish.
This can be a bit of a bland way of cooking on its own. There are some good recipes for cooking fish in parcels in the oven. These will not make your kitchen smell 'fishy' for days. Here is one:

Mediterranean Fish with roast potatoes

Time: 10 minutes preparation, 25 minutes cooking.

Serves 2

- **oil** for potatoes
- 3 large **potatoes**, cut into 1" cubes
- 2 **cod** or **haddock steaks**
- 6 **olives**, chopped
- juice of ½ **lemon**
- 2 **tomatoes**, chopped
- 1 clove **garlic**, finely chopped
- ¼ **red pepper**, finely chopped
- **salt** and **pepper**

1. Preheat the oven to 180ºC fan oven/200ºC/Gas 6.
2. Mix together the olives, tomatoes, lemon juice, garlic and peppers.
3. Put the potatoes on a baking tray, drizzle with oil and season with salt. Using your hands, make sure the oil is evenly distributed. Place in the oven.
4. Prepare a piece of foil, large enough to wrap both pieces of fish. It is best if you double the foil. Place on a baking tray, or flat casserole dish.
5. Put the fish on the foil and pile the tomato mixture equally on each piece of fish. Season well with salt and pepper. Fold up the parcels, pinching the joins together to seal. Place in the oven for 20 - 25 minutes, depending on the thickness of the steaks.
6. Check that the potatoes are not getting too browned, but if so, turn them on the tray.
7. Everything should be cooked at the same time. Take the fish out of the parcels and spoon the juices over the fish. Serve with the mini roasts.

Sauces

Question 78

> "What sauces would you recommend to cook with a steak and what sauces can you make yourself?"
>
> *Christopher Corbett*

Creamy Mustard sauce

for 2 people

2 tablespoons **crème fraîche** or **soured cream**

1 tablespoon **wholegrain mustard**

Just stir the 2 ingredients together!

Honey Mustard Sauce

- 1 **onion**, finely chopped
- 1½ teaspoons grated **ginger**
- ½ teaspoon **cumin**
- ½ teaspoon **cinnamon**
- 1 teaspoon **flour**
- 1 tablespoon **honey**
- 1 dessertspoon **wholegrain mustard**
- ⅓ mug **water**
- **salt** and **pepper**
- **oil** to fry

1. Heat a little oil in a pan and fry the onion and ginger.
2. Add the flour and cook for 30 seconds, stirring well.
3. Add the rest of the ingredients and bring to the boil.
4. Turn down to simmer, for 2 minutes.

Balsamic and onion Sauce

- 2 **onions**, cut into wedges
- 1 tablespoon **oil**
- 1 tablespoon **balsamic vinegar**
- 1 tablespoon **brown sugar**
- **salt** and **pepper**

1. Heat the oil in a pan and add the onions until they become quite brown. The caramelization of the onions adds to the flavour. This may take 4 - 5 minutes, stirring frequently
2. Once the onions are browned, add the balsamic vinegar and sugar and season well. Bring to the boil, turn down the heat and simmer for 2 - 3 minutes.

Question 79

"What easy alternatives to tomatoes can I use in meat sauce?"

Matthew Atkinson

Depends on what kind of meat you are using. If you are using minced beef, then tomato sauce is the best. If you are using chicken, you can make a simple sauce by just adding double cream to fried onions and chicken. See the Creamy Chicken recipe on page 19.

Here is another you could try:

Mushroom sauce

for 2 people

- **oil** to fry
- 1 **onion**, finely chopped
- 5 **mushrooms**, sliced
- 1 teaspoon **flour**
- 1 mug of **milk** or **cream**
- 1 **vegetable stock cube**
- **salt** and **pepper**

1. Heat a little oil in a pan and fry the onions and mushrooms, until they are beginning to brown.
2. Add the flour and stir well.
3. Add the milk/cream and stock cube and bring to the boil, stirring frequently. The sauce should thicken. Season well with salt and pepper.

Question 80

Tomato and Basil Sauce

- 1 **onion**, sliced
- 400g **tin tomatoes**
- 2 tablespoon fresh **basil**, chopped
- 1 teaspoon freshly ground **black pepper**
- 1 tablespoon **tomato purée**
- 1 tablespoon **white wine vinegar**
- 1 teaspoon **sugar**
- **oil** to fry

1. Heat a little oil in a pan and fry the onions until they begin to brown.
2. Add the rest of the ingredients and bring to the boil. You can use as it is, or blitz with a hand-held blender.
3. You can serve on its own with pasta, or add some chopped-up ham or salami.

Cheese Sauce

- o 1 mug grated **cheese**
- o pinch of **paprika**
- o 1 tablespoon **flour**
- o 1 mug **milk**
- o 1 teaspoon **mustard**
- o 1 teaspoon **butter**
- o **salt** and **pepper**

1. Mix the cheese, paprika and flour in a saucepan.
2. Make sure that the flour is evenly distributed.
3. Add the milk and the mustard and stir well. Add the butter.
4. Bring to the boil and stir frequently, especially as the sauce begins to boil. It should thicken. Season with salt and pepper.
5. If you add this to pasta, you could also add some chopped up ham, or just chopped fresh tomatoes.

Pepper sauce

- 1½ **red peppers**, chopped
- ½ **onion**, chopped
- 1 clove **garlic**, chopped
- ½ teaspoon **sugar**
- 1 tablespoon **cream**
- **salt** and **pepper**

1. Fry the chopped peppers, onions, and garlic in a saucepan, over a medium heat, for 5-8 minutes until they are really soft. Add the sugar.
2. Use the hand-held blender to liquidize.
3. Add the cream and season well with salt and freshly ground black pepper. You can add half a teaspoon of chilli powder, if you like.

Pesto sauce

Pesto is made from basil, pine nuts and parmesan cheese. You can make the sauce from these fresh ingredients but a jar of the ready-made stuff is very convenient for students.

- 2 tablespoons ready-made **green pesto sauce**
- 3 tablespoons **double cream**

1. Just mix these two ingredients together and add to the cooked, warm pasta.
2. If you have some leftover roast chicken (see page 111) this would be a great way to use it. Just cut into small pieces and add with the pesto sauce.

Tagliatelli

Penne

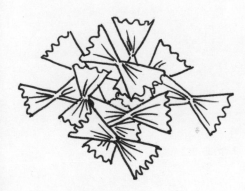

farfalle

Conchiglie

When Things
Go Wrong...

Question 81

> "What should I do if I have added too much chilli powder to a meal?" *Jacob Padley*

We have all done this at one time or another. We get a little carried away with the chilli powder and all of a sudden the food is inedible. There are, however, some ways to cool the food down, but you will need to add more ingredients to the dish.

If it is a chilli dish, then add another **tin of tomatoes** and, maybe, another **tin of beans**.

If you have added too much curry powder, or paste, one way to dilute the strong taste is to add a **cut up potato** and allow it to cook for 10 minutes. It should absorb some of the flavour.

Stirring in some **yogurt**, to a curry that is too hot, will also help.

If it is a Thai dish, you could try adding some lime juice, or more **coconut milk** (if it is in the recipe).

If it is a 'creamy' dish, then **add more cream.**

Question 82

The reason noodles stick together, is because they are overcooked. Cook them for the recommended time and no more. If you add noodles to a stir fry, add them just at the end and only heat them through. If the pan is quite hot, it will only take 30 seconds or so.

You can get many different types of noodles now. Ready-to-wok, or fresh noodles, are the easiest to use, as you do not need to pre-cook them. The dried noodles need to be soaked in boiling water for a few minutes and then added to the dish. Again, they do not need to be cooked for more than 30 seconds.

Rice noodles are probably the most difficult to cook, so make sure you don't try the really fine ones, get the thicker ones. They just need to be soaked in water for a few minutes.

If you are using noodles in a stir fry, it is best to add some kind of sauce to them to stop them sticking; hoisin, teriyaki or black bean, for example.

Question 83

"Is there anything I can do to salvage melted chocolate, when it seizes up and goes all bitty? I don't know if it's burnt and wasted or you can fix it..."   *Jess Gore*

Sorry, but if it has gone hard, there is usually no way back. You can try adding a little butter and see if it works. The separation is caused by heating the chocolate at too high a temperature. This causes the cocoa and the cocoa butter to separate.

If you just put chocolate straight into a saucepan, the heat is too intense. You need to melt chocolate very slowly. Here is a proven method:

1. Put the chocolate in a bowl and place it over a pan of simmering water. Make sure that the water does not touch the bottom of the bowl.
2. Stir the chocolate every now and then.
3. Once it has melted, carefully take the bowl off the pan (the bowl will be hot), and leave to cool a little, before putting it in your recipe.

water level not touching bowl

Question 84

"If a recipe asks for self-raising flour, but I only have plain, can I use this instead or do I need to add something?" *Beth Pattison*

If you use plain flour when the recipe states 'self-raising' than you will have very flat, solid, cakes.

Plain flour has no raising agent, so you would need to add approximately 1 teaspoon of baking powder, to every 8 oz of plain flour you use. This is only an approximate measure, as it really depends on what you are making.

Making Life Easier While Cooking

Question 85

"Are there any tips about keeping to time whilst cooking?"
Georgia

"What is the easiest way to get timings right when making a meal?"
Pippa Nelson

Many recipes will state that the meal should take 25 minutes to prepare. First, don't worry if you are a little slower, some people just work faster than others.

Read through the recipe first, so that you are clear what is supposed to happen and when.

One way not to panic, whilst cooking, is to get everything ready before you start. For instance, chop all the vegetables and have everything you need for the recipe out of the cupboards. If you are searching for things whilst you are trying to cook, you may burn the food etc.

If the recipe does not give you a clear order in which to do things, work out an order yourself.

Cooking should be enjoyable, not a stress. If you only have a little time, choose something that is really quick, or that you have cooked before and have confidence to cook.

Question 86

> "When cooking, how can you avoid making lots of washing up?" *Emily Norman*

Choose easy recipes.

Salads (not just boring lettuce and tomatoes), are quick to prepare and generally use less pots and pans. They can be very tasty and usually very healthy.

Cook more than one thing in a pan. For example, if you are cooking pasta and want to serve green beans with it, add the beans to the pan five minutes before the end of the cooking time of the pasta.

You can cook some foods in foil parcels, see page 150.

Choose one-pot dishes. There are lots of recipes where you just put things in a casserole and slow cook them. Here is one opposite, just a casserole dish is needed for the cooking. You do need to plan ahead, as the cooking time is longer.

one pot recipes

hob to oven casserole pots

Chicken Hot Pot

Serves 2   Preparation time 5 minutes, cooking time 1 hour 30 minutes

- 1 mug hot **water**
- 1 **chicken stock cube**
- 4 **chicken thighs**, skins removed
- 3 **carrots**, washed and sliced
- 3 large **potatoes**, washed and cut into chunks
- 1 **onion**, cut into 6 wedges
- 2 cloves **garlic**, chopped
- **salt** and **pepper**

1. Preheat oven to 190°C fan oven/220°C/Gas 7.
2. Put the stock cube in a mug, fill up with the hot water and stir until the cube has dissolved.
3. Put all the ingredients in a casserole dish, season with salt and pepper.
4. Pour the stock into the casserole dish.
5. Cover with a lid or foil, and cook for 1 hour 30 minutes.
6. You can take the lid off for the last half hour, to let things brown a little.

Question 87

"How do I work efficiently, to shorten the time it takes to cook my dinner?"

Matt Harrison

"What is the fastest way to produce a cooked meal?"

Brad Willingham

If you are a confident cook and familiar with the dish you are cooking, there are a few ways of going a bit faster.

Make sure you have a clear working space, working around mess always takes longer.

You can do some things in parallel. For instance, when I cook something like Spaghetti Bolognese, I will chop the onions, but halfway through, I would put the pan on to heat with the oil in. By the time I have finished chopping the onion, the oil is hot. While the onions are cooking, I will prepare the mince, then add to the pan at the appropriate time. While the mince cooks, I find the rest of the ingredients and add as necessary.

Halfway through this process, I would put the water on to boil, for the spaghetti.

This way, I prepare and cook in parallel. This is not a method I would recommend for an inexperienced cook.

Question 88

"Are you OK to cook a large batch of bolognese and freeze it? If so how long can you freeze it for?"   *Charlotte Maguiness*

This is a great idea. The Spaghetti Bolognese recipe is a basic one that you can add other things to when you reheat it. Chilli and beans, for example, can be added.

If you are cooking for yourself and not sharing with others, it make sense to cook enough for 2 meals and freeze the second portion.

Mince meals reheat well, as do some chicken hot pots and casseroles.

In theory, once you freeze something, it could last for years. In practice, some foods degrade in the freezer and lose their taste and texture. I would say 6 months is a good limit for most foods in the freezer.

Question 89

> "What is healthy, nutritious, but takes little time to cook and requires little preparation?"
>
> *Henry Curran*

> "What dish do I need the least utensils to make?"
>
> *Aseem Mishra*

This meal takes very little time to prepare, but you do need to leave 25 minutes for it to cook in the oven. It also requires no pots and pans for you to wash up. Just the foil to throw away!

Chicken meal in a parcel

Serves 1

- 1 large **potato**, cut into ¼" slices
- 1 **chicken breast**
- 1" cube of **butter**
- juice of a ½ **lemon**
- ½ **onion**, thinly sliced
- 1 **tomato**, cut into ¼'s
- ½ **courgette**, sliced
- ½ teaspoon **mixed dried herbs**
- **salt** and **pepper**
- foil

1. Preheat the oven to 180°C fan oven/200°C/Gas 6.
2. Prepare a double sheet of foil to make a parcel. Place it on a baking tray.
3. Place the potatoes in the middle of the sheet. Put the chicken breast on top of the potatoes.
4. Put the courgette, onions and tomatoes in the parcel.
5. Sprinkle on the herbs and the lemon juice. Season well.
6. Seal the parcel by scrunching the foil together and place in the oven for 25 minutes.

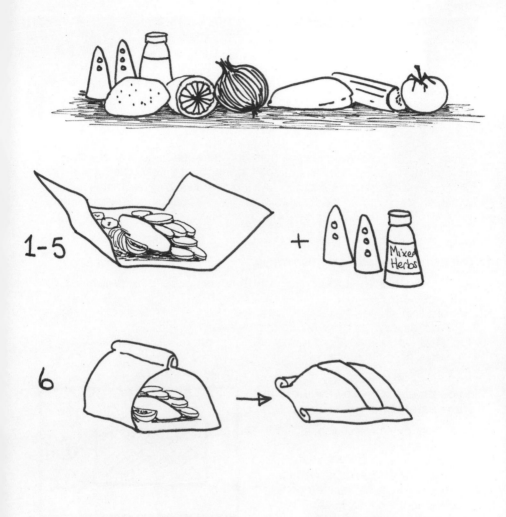

1-5 +

6

6a

180°c fan oven
200°C
gas 6

25 minutes

Question 90

> ## "What shouldn't you cook in a microwave? What are the best things to cook in a microwave?"
>
> *Elliot Hodges*

Personally, I think microwaves are there only for speed and convenience. I think they are great for baking potatoes, popcorn, defrosting and reheating food, or heating convenience food. As the microwave cooks things very quickly, it does not give the flavours in the food a chance to develop. Often meats and eggs become rubbery in a microwave.

Many may disagree with me.

Things never to put in a microwave:

- Eggs in their shells, or an egg yolk that has not been pierced, as it will explode.
- Shellfish will go very rubbery, as it takes very little time to cook on the hob. No time is saved by using the microwave.
- Steak. If you can afford to buy steak, do not ruin it in the microwave, see page 103.

If you do use a microwave here are some safety tips:

- Never put in metal dishes or containers.
- Pierce lids.
- If you reheat liquids, soups for example, stir halfway through, to ensure it is evenly heated.
- Let the food stand for 1 minute. After it comes out, it can be extremely hot.

Question 91

"What is the easiest type of meat to cook?"
Charlotte Ironside

It is not so much which meat is easiest, rather, how you cook the meat and which recipe you choose.

For instance, mince is very easy to cook with, when you make Spaghetti Bolognese, Hot Pots, Chilli etc. If all you eat is mince, you will soon get bored.

Chicken breasts are easy to cook with, as they cook quickly. They are a little more expensive, but you can make one spread out to feed two people, by adding a few more vegetables. See Creamy Chicken page 19.

Chicken thighs can also be easy, but need a longer cooking time. See the Chicken Hot Pot on page 147.

Question 92

> "Scenario. I'm in a rush, need to get out at night time. What meal can I cook in the shortest time possible that's warm and not from a microwave?
> What examples of quick meals can be made in a rush?"
>
> *Michael Pearson, Sam Morris and John Norrie*

Here is a Chicken Noodle recipe. It is a much healthier and nutritious version of pot noodle and takes only minutes longer to cook.

Chicken Noodles Serves 1 Total time 10 minutes

- ¼ x 250g pack of **egg noodles**
- one **chicken breast** or three small **chicken fillets**
- **oil** to fry
- 2 **spring onions**, sliced
- ¼ **red pepper**
- ½ **chicken stock cube**, dissolved in ½ mug **boiling water**
- 1 teaspoon **soy** or **hoisin sauce**
- **salt** and **pepper**

1. Cover the noodles with boiling water and leave to stand for 4 minutes.
2. Cut the chicken into bite size pieces and fry in the oil.
3. Add the onion and pepper and fry for 2 minutes.
4. Mix the stock and the soy or hoisin sauce together with the drained noodles and cook for 30 seconds.
5. Serve.

Miscellaneous

Question 93

"Best foods to have at a BBQ?" *Joe Midgley*

Make your BBQs something more than the standard cheap burgers and plastic cheese squares. Below, I give a guide to planning a BBQ. Get friends to pitch in on the preparation and make sure the person cooking at the barbeque can cook!

A trick to avoiding disasters is to never cook things over a flame, as they will burn on the outside, before they are cooked through. Wait until the flames have died down and you just have hot coals. Be patient. Don't be tempted to put things on to cook before this point.

Another tip is to use a BBQ with a lid. It will act like an oven and keep heat around what you are cooking. This will help with cooking meat all the way through.

Once you know the approximate number of people coming to the BBQ, choose from the selection below. Depending on appetites, allow 4 - 5 meat portions per person and 3 - 4 salad portions per person.

BBQ Tips

Make sure everything is prepared before you begin to cook on the BBQ. It is best to do a BBQ with a few helpers. Half the fun is preparing together and everyone wants a go at the cooking.

Sausages usually contain a lot of fat which drips down onto the BBQ and will cause flames and burnt food. The idea is not to have flames licking the food.

If you cook all the same type of food at one time, it is easier to assess the right cooking times. This way, food will be neither undercooked nor overcooked.

Burgers - much better than bought ones!

- 1 kg **beef** mince
- 1 **egg**, beaten
- 1 **onion**, finely chopped
- 6 pieces of **sun-dried tomatoes**, chopped finely
- **salt** and **pepper**

1. Mix everything together, really well, with your hands, to make the mixture as smooth as possible.
2. Form into burgers. Don't make them too big, as this will make it easier to ensure that they are cooked right through.

Chicken pieces

- 6 **chicken breasts**
- 2 tablespoons **soy sauce**
- 2 teaspoons grated fresh **ginger**
- 2 tablespoons **oil**
- 1 tablespoon **honey**

1. Cut the chicken breasts, lengthways, into 3 pieces. This makes it easier to ensure that the meat is cooked through.
2. Mix together the rest of the ingredients to form a marinade. Add the chicken, cover with cling film and leave for 2 hours in the fridge.

Potato wedges

12 large potatoes, cut into wedges

1. Preheat the oven to 200°C fan oven/220°C/Gas 7.
2. Place the potatoes on a baking tray, drizzle with oil and season with salt and pepper.
3. Place in the oven when the BBQ is just about ready to cook on. Cook for 25 minutes. It may be better to cook 2 trays at a time. In this way, you have a supply of freshly cooked wedges throughout the BBQ.

Chicken Kebabs

- 4 **chicken breasts**, each breast cut into 6
- 4 **red onions**, each cut into 6 wedges
- 6 **tomatoes**, cut in 4s
- 12 **mushrooms**, cut in half
- 3 **red peppers**, cut into 12 pieces each
- **wooden skewers**

Marinade

- 2 tablespoons **soy**
- 1 tablespoon **sugar**
- 2 tablespoons **oil**
- 1 tablespoon **honey**
- 1 tablespoon chopped fresh **basil**
- **salt** and **pepper**

1. Mix the marinade ingredients in a large bowl and add the chicken. Leave for 1 hour.
2. Soak the wooden skewers in water, this should stop them burning too much when you BBQ them.
3. Distribute all the ingredients across the skewers (around 9 pieces per skewer).
4. When you BBQ, make sure the chicken is cooked all the way through by testing a large piece.

Rice Salad

makes enough for 12 to have a portion.

- 1 mug **rice**, cooked in 2 mugs water with 1 teaspoon **pilau rice seasoning** (See page 86)
- 340g can **sweetcorn**, drained
- 2 green **eating apples**, cored and cut into small chunks
- handful of **sultanas** or **raisins**
- 6 spring **onions**, chopped
- 2 tablespoons chopped fresh **basil**

Once the rice has cooled just mix everything together

Question 94

"What can you cook with beer (as an ingredient, not just cooking while drinking...)?"

Dan Richter

Here is a great recipe to cook with beer. Same rule applies to cooking with wine, i.e. if you would not drink it, don't cook with it. So don't put any old cheap stuff in!

Beef in Ale with Cheddar & Mustard Mash and Carrots

Serves 6

- 12 **shallot onions** (whole) or 2 onions, cut into wedges
- oil to fry
- 1 kg **stewing beef**, cut into bite-size pieces
- 2 tablespoons **flour**
- 500ml bottle of **fruity ale**
- 2 tablespoons **liquid beef stock** or 2 **beef stock cubes** or **stock pots**
- **salt** and **pepper**

Mash

- 10 medium **potatoes**
- 3 x1" cubes **butter**
- 1 mug grated **cheddar cheese**
- 1 tablespoon **wholegrain mustard**
- 12 **carrots**
- 2 x 1" cubes **butter** to cook

1. Preheat the oven to 180°C fan oven/200°C/Gas 6.
2. In a large pan or wok, fry the onions (or shallots) in a little oil until they begin to brown. Add the meat to the pan. You may need a little more oil at this point. Cook until the meat is no longer red. Stir frequently.
3. Add the flour and stir well to distribute evenly. Add the ale and the stock. Season well with salt and pepper. Stir well and bring to the boil. The sauce should thicken slightly, but will thicken a lot more in the oven as it cooks. Transfer to a casserole dish, putting a lid or foil on to cover. Cook in the oven for 1½ hours. After 1 hour, give it a stir to make sure it is not sticking to the bottom of the dish. Add a little more water if the sauce is getting too thick.
4. About 35 minutes before the end of the cooking time, prepare the carrots. Peel and cut into rings. Put in an ovenproof dish and add 2 x 1" cubes of butter and ½ mug water, together with plenty of salt and pepper. Cover the dish with some foil and bake in the oven for about 30 minutes.
5. While the carrots are cooking, put the water on to boil for the mash. Peel the potatoes and cut them into 2" chunks. Put them in the boiling water and bring back to the boil. Turn down and simmer for 10 - 15 minutes until tender. Drain and return to the pan. Add the butter, cheese and mustard and mash. Leave with the lid on until needed.
6. Serve the beef in ale with the mash and carrots.

Question 95

"What does 'cream the butter and sugar' mean?"

Eleanor Cowan-Rawcliffe

Creaming the butter and sugar is simply transforming the separate ingredients into a creamy mixture. Here's how:

Place in a good size bowl and beat together, either with a wooden spoon - this will give you a good workout - or with some electric beaters. It is best to start with butter which has been out of the fridge for a couple of hours, in order to make it soft. Butter straight from the fridge is difficult even for electric beaters.

When it is creamed, the butter and sugar should be quite light in colour and in consistency.

You will need to 'cream butter and sugar' for many cookie and cake recipes. There is one to try on the oposite page:

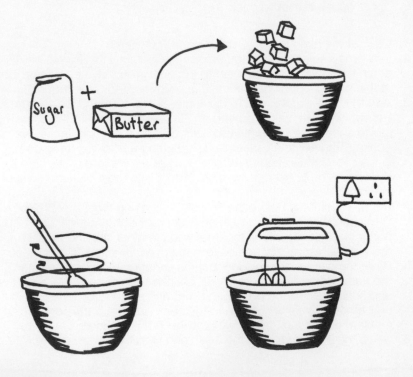

Chocolate Chip Cookies

These cookies are delicious, crunchy on the outside and a bit gooey on the inside. Don't skimp on the butter and use margarine, it won't taste nearly as good!

Makes 16   **Preparation time 15 minutes, cooking time 10 - 12 minutes.**

- ½ x 250g packet of **butter**
- 1 mug of soft **brown sugar**
- 1 large **egg**
- 1 teaspoon of **vanilla extract**
- 1 x 100g packet of **chocolate chips**, ½ **milk** and ½ **white** works well.
- 1½ mugs **self-raising flour**

1. Preheat the oven to 180°C fan oven/200°C/Gas 6. Grease 2 baking trays. If you only have one tray, you can cook them in two batches. The mixture will be OK to leave ½, while the other ½ cooks.

2. Mix the butter and sugar together and beat well. Add the egg and the vanilla extract. Beat well.

3. Add the chocolate chips and mix, then add the flour and mix well. The cookie dough will be quite stiff. Tip onto a floured surface and squash into a long sausage. Do not knead the dough, in fact, handle it as little as possible. Cut into 16 and roll each portion into a ball. Then squash each ball, so it is about ½" thick and approximately 2½" across. Place on the baking tray.

4. Put in the oven and bake for 10 - 12 minutes. The cookies do not need to brown, just be crisp on the outside. Leave to cool for a few minutes. The cookies should be a little soft on the inside.

If you want to make double Chocolate Chip Cookies, then replace 2 tablespoons of the flour with 2 tablespoons of drinking chocolate.

Question 96

"How do you zest a lemon?" *Henry Curran*

Wash the lemon and then grate the yellow part of the skin on the fine side of the grater. Make sure you don't get any of the pith (white bit), as it can be quite bitter.

You can use the zest of a lemon in some salad dressings, or, for example, in baking cheesecakes.

Easy Lemon Cheesecake

Serves 4

- 250g packet of **digestive biscuits**
- ¼ x 500g pack of **butter**
- 1 mug of **double cream**
- 2 tablespoons **white sugar**
- 250g packet of **cream cheese**
- rind and juice of a **lemon**
- **fruit to decorate**, e.g. oranges or strawberries

1. Put the digestive biscuits into a polythene bag and crush them with a rolling pin, milk bottle, or tin of beans. There should be no lumps left, just crumbs!
2. Melt the butter in a saucepan and add the crushed biscuit. Mix well.
3. Press the biscuit mixture into the bottom of a 20 cm loose-bottomed cake tin.
4. Beat the cream and sugar together with a whisk until the cream thickens. Don't keep beating once it has thickened, or it will turn to butter.
5. Gently fold in the cream cheese, grated lemon rind and juice. The lemon juice is essential, as it helps the cream to set. Pour on to the top of the biscuit mixture and gently spread out.
6. Leave in the fridge for 4 hours to set.
7. Once the cheesecake has set, loosen the side with a knife and place the loose bottomed tin on a jam jar or tin and push the sides down.
8. Decorate the top with fruit.

Question 97

> ## "How can you make a plain salad taste really nice?"
>
> *Grace Shoebridge*

There are lots of different kinds of salad dressing that you can buy. One way to make a simple French Salad dressing is to mix the following together:

- 1 tablespoon olive oil
- 1 tablespoon lemon juice or wine vinegar
- 1 teaspoon sugar
- salt and pepper

Here is a really tasty tuna salad using another lovely, simple salad dressing.

Tuna Salad

Time: 15 minutes. Serves 2

Dressing

- 200g tin **tuna** in oil, drained of oil
- **bistro salad** or **lettuce**
- ¼ **cucumber**, cut into chunks
- 4 **spring onions**
- 12 **olives**, cut into pieces
- 3 **tomatoes**, cut into wedges
- fresh crusty **bread** to serve.

- 2 tablespoons **mayo**
- 1 tablespoon **olive oil**
- juice of a **lemon**
- 1 dessertspoon **wholegrain mustard**
- **salt** and **pepper**

1. Put enough bistro salad in a bowl for 2 people.
2. Add the cucumber, onions, olives and tomatoes.
3. Tip the tuna out of the tin into a bowl and break up into pieces. Add to the salad and gently mix all the ingredients together. Divide between the 2 plates.
4. Mix all the dressing ingredients together and drizzle over the salads.
5. Serve with crusty bread or ciabatta.

> **"When should dressing be put on salad, as it often goes soggy and limp?"**
>
> *Reece Taylor*

Don't add the dressing until just before you serve it. The vinegar or lemon juice in the dressing causes the greens in the salad to wilt and not be too appetizing.

Question 98

"What's the translation between gas mark and temperature?"   *Sam Morris*

Usually, in the UK, you have either electric, Centigrade ovens, or gas ovens. The electric ovens vary in temperature distribution, whilst the fan assisted ovens circulate the heat around the food and cook it evenly and more quickly. This means the temperature in a fan assisted oven needs to be a little lower than a normal Centigrade oven. Here is a conversion chart:

Question 99

> "What is the best meal to cook for a date and why?"
> *James Gould*
>
> "What is the easiest romantic meal to cook?"
> *James Harwood*

When cooking for a date, it is best to do something easy, that you know will work and that does not involve you standing in the kitchen for most of the evening. You do want to try to produce something a bit impressive and away from the ordinary. As you are a student, budget is also part of the equation.

Here is a suggestion for a meal and dessert you could try. It is easy and not too expensive, but will look great.

Prepare all the ingredients and the sauce for the Lemon Chicken beforehand, then, when your date arrives, it will be so easy to cook. You can make the Tiramisu earlier in the day.

Lemon Chicken

Serves 2   **Preparation and cooking time 15 minutes**

Sauce

- 1 dessertspoon **cornflour**
- ¾ mug cold **water**
- juice of a **lemon**
- 3 dessertspoons **sugar**

- 1 mug **basmati rice** + 2 mugs **water**
- 1 teaspoon **pilau rice seasoning**
- 1 **lemon**
- 2 spring **onions**
- **oil** to fry
- 2 whole **chicken breasts**

1. Bring the two mugs of water to the boil. Add the rice and the pilau rice seasoning. Bring back to the boil, then turn down to simmer, with the lid on, for 12 - 15 minutes, until all the water has been absorbed and the rice is tender. Leave to one side until needed.
2. Mix the sauce ingredients together until smooth. Slice the other lemon. Cut the spring onions into small strips.
3. Heat a little oil in the frying pan. Add the whole chicken breasts. Cook on a high heat for 2 minutes each side. Turn the heat down to medium and cook for a further 4 minutes each side, with a lid on. Check to see that the meat is cooked through. If it is, remove from the pan and place on a serving dish.
4. Stir the sauce ingredients again and then add to the pan. Stir until the sauce comes to the boil. It should thicken. Add the slices of lemon and heat them over a gentle heat for 1 minute. Take off the heat.
5. Cut the chicken breasts into slices. Arrange the lemon slices on top and pour the sauce over.
6. Serve with rice and vegetables. Mangetout or sugar snaps will go well with this dish.

Tiramisu

Serves 2   Preparation time 20 minutes, fridge time 1 hour.

- 1 tablespoon **instant coffee** + 3 tablespoons **water**
- 2 tablespoons **brandy** or **rum**
- ¼ x 175g pack **sponge fingers**
- 250g pot of **mascarpone cheese**
- ½ x 425g **tin custard**
- 1 tablespoon **icing sugar**
- **cocoa powde**r to finish

1. Mix the coffee with the water and alcohol. Dip the sponge fingers in the liquid and use them to line the bottom of a bowl. If you do not have a glass bowl, a casserole dish will do.
2. Soften the mascarpone cheese with a spoon and mix in the custard and sugar until it is smooth. Pile on top of the sponge fingers.
3. Leave to set for about 1 hour and then sprinkle cocoa on the top.

Question 100

"What's the best meal to cure a hangover?"
Will Overvoorde

"What is the best food to cure a hangover?"
Jodie Brumhead

Dehydration is the main cause for the nasty effects of a hangover. Alcohol is a diuretic, therefore you have lost lots of water from your body. Nausea and abdominal pains are a result of the alcohol irritating your stomach lining.

One way to avoid the hangover, is to alternate the alcoholic drinks with non-fizzy soft drinks. Fizzy drinks increase the amount of alcohol going into your blood stream.

Once you have the hangover, here are a few suggestions:

1. Don't drink coffee or caffeine drinks.
2. 'Hair of the dog' is not a good idea, just prolongs the agony.
3. Take antacid remedies, such as Alka Seltzer, ibruprofen or paracetemol, for the headache.
4. Rest and try to get some sleep.
5. Drink lots of water and juice, preferably something containing vitamin C. Have a vitamin C drink or a sports drink.
6. If you can face it, have a couple of eggs on toast. Eggs contain cysteine, which is thought to absorb the destructive chemicals heading for your liver.

Question 101

Eat a good meal before you go out. Not too healthy, but a fatty meal, on this occasion, is good. Have a drink of milk. The fat helps to protect your stomach lining.

Before you go to bed, drink lots of water (at least 1 pint) and take some vitamin C (in juice or tablets). Maybe have a slice of toast.

Silly
Questions

> ## "How do you kill a mockingbird, 'cos the book is a massive disappointment?"
>
> *Jonathan Briscoe*

Well, I am sorry about the book. Having looked at the mockingbird, I would not want to kill it

> ## "How do they put the holes in cheese?"
>
> *James Upshal*

Apparently, it is the gassy bacteria that the Swiss put in Emmental, that makes those wonderful holes. The bubbles of gas are produced during manufacture as the cheese warms and these gas bubbles become holes in the cheese. Technically the holes are called 'eyes'.

Enjoy a bit of Emmental!

"How do I avoid chopping my fingers off?"

Rob Dalziel

Just keep them tucked in Rob and be careful. If you are especially accident prone have the number of A & E handy and should you chop off your finger, remember to take it with you!

"How long do you cook squirrel for?"

A Merrick

Let me know when you find out please, I am sure I could write a recipe book for squirrel cooking.

"What foods can make you taller?"
Kyle Daniel

Don't have a definitive answer to this, but Chinese people in the north of China are much taller than those in the south. One reason may be their diet; they eat much more red meat and bread and drink more milk. This is not a proven theory and it may be too late for you Kyle.

"What is the best way to cook octopus?"
Simon Hammersley

Apparently, you can boil it for a long time, grill it or fry it. The choice is yours Simon, but don't tell anyone I recommended it.

> "How do you make pink custard?"
>
> *Isra Rehman*

Add a bit of red food colouring.

> "Why is it that every time I go out and have a drink, I always crave a kebab?"
>
> *Joshua Clements*

Maybe, it is your body telling you that you need to line your stomach before drinking? Or, maybe, you just like kebabs, Josh.

> "What's better for me, yesterday's Pizza Hut or today's McDonald's? *Joshua Clements*

Do you really want me to get sued by either of these establishments?

> "Can you cook with beetles? What do they taste like? Are there any bad side effects?" *Matt Bentley*

You can dry roast them in the oven for 2 hours. They will then be crisp, so crush them and add them to your favourite soup. When you have tried this Matt, let me know how it tastes and if you had any bad side effects.

George and Henrietta have guided you through 101 questions. George was our beloved cat, who was full of attitude and curiosity. I thought I would make up a little companion for George and he was such a fan of chickens that Henrietta seemed like the logical choice to have as his buddy.

NOTES

NOTES

NOTES

A

asparagus 78
avoid washing up 146

B

baked apples 62
baked potatoes 74
balsamic and onion sauce
131
bbq 157
beef
beef in ale with mash 161
burgers 57, 158
cooking steak 102
when is it cooked 125
beef in ale with cheddar &
mustard mash and carrots
161
beef steak, how to cook 102
beef steak with mash and
mustard sauce 103
beef, when is it cooked 124
beer, cooking with 160
before a night out, what to eat
173
boil an egg 94
breaded chicken, when is it
cooked 128
breaded fish, when is it
cooked 128
breakfast, healthy 58
brown rice 87
budget
equipment 10
weekly/daily meals 15
budget for equipment 12
budget for food 15
burgers 57, 158

C

cheapest meats 18

cheese sauce 134
cheesy croutons 109
chicken curry 117
chicken fried rice 100
chicken hot pot 147
chicken, how to cook 110
chicken kebabs 159
chicken meal in a parcel 150
chicken pieces, bbq 158
chicken, when is it cooked
124
chickpea patties 22
chillies, chopping 82
chilli powder, too much 139
chocolate chip cookies 163
chocolate, melting 141
chocolate sauce 112
chopping onions 76
chopping vegetables 80
cooking for a date 169
cooking in a hurry 154
cooking oil 69
cooking veg 79
cost per meal 16
couscous, how to cook 115
cracking eggs 89
creaming butter and sugar
162
creamy chicken 19
creamy mustard sauce 131

D

defrosting 33
dressing, when to put on 167

E

easiest meat to cook 153
efficient cooking 148
eggie bread 91
eggs
boil an egg 94

eggie bread 91
fried eggs 90
how long to keep 96
omelettes 92
poaching an egg 93
scrambled eggs 95
eggs, cracking 89
equipment needed 10
exploding potatoes 74

F

fast cooking 148
fisherman's pie 25
fish, when is it cooked 125
food poisoning 35
food that is past it 42
freezing food 31
freezing spaghetti bolognese 149
french onion soup 109
fresh or frozen veg 55
fried eggs 90
fruit salad 63

G

gas mark translation 168
good and bad fridge 50
green potatoes 39

H

hangover, cure 172
healthy cooking methods 66
healthy burgers 57
healthy chips 56
healthy desserts 62
healthy snack 71
herbs and spices 29
high protein food 70
hoisin noodles 99
home-made curry 117

honey mustard sauce 131
how long to keep eggs 96
how long to keep things 44
how to cook 6

I

ice cream 114
impressive meal 17

J

jacket potato 74

L

lamb, when is it cooked 124
leftovers 46
lemon cheesecake 165
lemon chicken 170

M

marinade 159
mash potatoes 73
meal before a night out 173
meat
    cheapest 18
    easiest 153
    red or white 61
mediterranean fish with roast potatoes 129
menu 15
microwave cooking 152
mince, how to cook 120
mouldy cheese 49
mushroom sauce 132
mustard mash 161

N

noodles, seasoning 99
noodles, stopping sticking together 140

nutritional and cheap 20

O

oils 68
omelettes 92
one-pot cooking 147
onions chopping 76
onions making you cry 76
oven temperatures 168

P

pancakes 101
pan roast a chicken 110
pasta, cooking 85
pepper sauce 135
pesto sauce 136
pizza, when is it cooked 127
poached chicken 67
poached egg 93
poached fish 67
pork, when is it cooked 124
potato wedges 56

Q

quick to cook 150
quorn 60

R

raw materials, looking after 43
raw meat 125
red of white meat 61
red or white onion 76
'reduced to clear' chicken 48
reheating food 37
reheating rice 36
rice, brown or white 87
rice, cooking 86
rice salad 159
roast dinner 104

roasting a chicken 111
roast potatoes 118
roast potatoes and sausages 106
romantic meal 169

S

salad, making them tasty 166
sauces 131-136
sausages and bacon, how to cook 116
sausages, when are they cooked 126
scrambled egg 95
self-raising flour 142
sharpening a knife 14
shepherd's pie 120
shopping tips 27
silly questions 174
smelly freezer 52
soup 108
spicy, cooling food down 139
store cupboard essentials 28
storing food 40
sunday lunch experience in halls 106
supermarket 27
sweet and sour chicken 17

T

takeaways 46
things not to reheat 38
timings when cooking 145
tinned fruit 65
tiramisu 171
tomato and basil sauce 133
tuna salad 166

U

utensils, cooking without lots of 150

V

vegetables, chopping 80
vegetable soup 108
victoria sponge 113

W

when is food cooked 123
white fish on a budget 24
white or brown bread 64
why cook 7

Z

zesting a lemon 164

Acknowledgements

Design - Ben May @ www.milkbottledesigns.co.uk

Design and Layout - Tim May

Editing - Ron May

Proof Reading - Fran Maciver

Thanks to all the students who have given us brilliant questions and a special thanks to Dan Richter, who has to qualify as our best contributor. May you all eat safely and well and graduate happily.

101 QUESTIONS STUDENTS ASK ABOUT COOKING

BY JOY MAY

Author: Joy May

1st Printed June 2010

ISBN: 0-9543179-6-3

ISBN: 978-0-9543179-6-6

Published by:

inTRADE (GB) Ltd, 24 Beverley Crescent, Bedford, Bedfordshire, MK40 4BY, UK

Contact: joymay@mac.com

Other books by Joy May

"Nosh 4 Students"

"Vegetarian Nosh 4 Students"

"Nosh for Graduates"